The Colored Aristocracy of St. Louis

The Colored Aristocracy of St. Louis

by Cyprian Clamorgan

Edited with an Introduction
by Julie Winch

University of Missouri Press
Columbia

University of Missouri Press, Columbia, Missouri 65211
Printed and bound in the United States of America

First paperback printing, 2018.

Library of Congress Cataloging-in-Publication Data

Clamorgan, Cyprian, b. 1830

The colored aristocracy of St. Louis / by Cyprian Clamorgan ; edited with an introduction by Julie Winch.

p. cm.

Includes bibliographical references (p.) and index.

ISBN 978-0-8262-2151-3 (paperback : alk. paper)

1. Free Afro-Americans—Missouri—Saint Louis—Social conditions—19th century. 2. Elite (Social sciences)—Missouri—Saint Louis—History—19th century. 3. Saint Louis (Mo.)—Social conditions—19th century. 4. Saint Louis (Mo.)—Race relations. 5. Clamorgan, Cyprian, b. 1830. I. Winch, Julie, 1953– . II. Title.

F474.S29N424 1999
305.896077866—dc21 99-29777
CIP

♾™ This paper meets the requirements of the American National Standard for Permanence of Paper for Printed Library Materials, Z39.48, 1984.

Typeface: Minion

To Roy Stuart Winch

Contents

Acknowledgments

I would like to begin by thanking Stephen Haas and Joel Fowler, the reference librarians at the Healey Library at the University of Massachusetts at Boston. My requests for information and for sources never defeated them. Thanks are also due to the staff of the New England Historic Genealogical Society, who diligently processed my orders for innumerable reels of microfilm. The research staff at the Missouri Historical Society were unfailingly gracious and resourceful. It was truly a pleasure to work at the MHS. Thomas Gruenenfelder of the St. Louis City Archives provided copies (in record time) of many of the documents without which this book could not have been written. Donna Carl Dahl, the archivist of the Alexian Brothers' Provincial Archives in Elk Grove Village, Illinois, kindly tracked down for me the details of Cyprian Clamorgan's last years in St. Louis. Anton Pregaldin, of Clayton, Missouri, generously shared with me his work on the old French families of St. Louis. Kathryn Silva, a History Honors student at the University of Massachusetts at Boston, spent days poring over microfilms of the St. Louis city directories at the Boston Public Library. Hopefully, that has not deterred her from going on to do graduate work in history. I would also like to thank the University of Massachusetts at Boston for providing a stipend for research. Professor James Brewer Stewart of Macalaster College read an early draft of my manuscript and suggested a number of revisions, as well as offering encouragement. I would also like to express my appreciation to the two anonymous readers for the University of Missouri Press for their insightful comments.

To my companion, Louis Cohen, I owe a tremendous debt of gratitude. Without him to encourage me, to listen as I tried to make sense of the lives of Cyprian Clamorgan and his contemporaries—and to fix my computer—this book could not have been written.

The Colored Aristocracy of St. Louis

Abbreviations

LDS	Church of Jesus Christ of Latter-Day Saints
MHS	Missouri Historical Society
MSA	Massachusetts State Archives
SLGS	St. Louis Genealogical Society

Introduction

To be a free man or woman of color in antebellum America was to be an anomaly. In a society that operated on the premise that all white people were free and all black people were enslaved, free people of African descent simply did not fit. In many parts of the South they were, from a legal standpoint, "slaves without masters." The law, and the vast majority of white southerners, assumed every black person was a slave unless he or she could prove otherwise. In some states in the lower South, free people of color needed white guardians to manage their affairs, represent them in all their dealings with state and local officials, conduct their business transactions, and hold their property for them. Although not technically slaves, they were far from "free." The situation in the North might have been rather better, but it was a question of degree. At some point almost every state above the Mason-Dixon Line contemplated ways of reducing the size of its black population, restricting black mobility, curtailing black political rights, limiting employment opportunities, and encouraging free people of color to emigrate to Africa. What the authorities could not accomplish, white mobs were often prepared to do by extralegal means.[1]

If the plight of the entire free community of color was an unenviable one, what was it like to be a member of what one African American writer referred to as the "higher classes of colored society"? To have money and

1. On southern free people see Ira Berlin, *Slaves without Masters: The Free Negro in the Antebellum South.* On their northern counterparts see Leon F. Litwack, *North of Slavery: The Negro in the Free States, 1790–1860* and James Oliver Horton and Lois E. Horton, *In Hope of Liberty: Culture, Community and Protest among Northern Free Blacks, 1700–1860.* On black urban life in the North and the South see Leonard P. Curry, *The Free Black in Urban America, 1800–1850: The Shadow of the Dream.* In addition to these studies, there is a growing body of scholarship on individual communities, and such aspects of community life as the growth of churches, employment opportunities, black education, the status of free women of color, and the role of the black press.

want the opportunity to make more? To want to enjoy the privileges that came with wealth? To have education and seek to use it? To want a role in the political process? To exert influence within the black community and want that influence recognized by the white community? In short, to be acknowledged for what one had achieved instead of for what one was in a society where to be of discernible African ancestry was to be forever excluded from the inner circles of power and prestige?[2]

Obviously, such concerns were far removed from the day-to-day existence of the vast majority of free people of color, whose lives were consumed, as were those of most whites, by the struggle to keep a roof over their heads, food on the table, clothes on their backs, and put a little aside to tide them over the crises that were sure to befall them—illness, unemployment, old age, the death of a breadwinner. And yet, in a very real sense, the fate of the men and women in the "higher classes of colored society" was inextricably bound up with that of the rest of their community. Restrictive legislation applied to all free people of color, regardless of wealth or education. White mobs vented their rage on well-dressed and affluent people of color as readily—and perhaps even more readily—than they did on poorer, less successful black people. In essence, white people relegated free people of color—*all* free people of color—to the lowest rung on the social ladder. If there was the occasional acknowledgment that the free black community had its "better sort," that was seldom translated into better treatment.

It was the notion that black people were all alike because they were black, that ancestry and phenotype somehow outweighed all other considerations, that Cyprian Clamorgan set out to challenge. Before the nation was engulfed in a bloody and protracted civil war, before all black men and women became "free" in law, if not in reality, he endeavored to convince white Americans that race was not an absolute, that the black community was not a monolith, that class, education, and especially wealth, should count for something.

2. Joseph Willson, *Sketches of the Higher Classes of Colored Society in Philadelphia by "A Southerner,"* 3. The focus of Willard B. Gatewood, Jr., in *Aristocrats of Color: The Black Elite, 1880–1920* is primarily on the post–Civil War era, but he does address the earlier period in the first chapter of his book. Litwack includes a brief analysis of class in his *North of Slavery* (179–86). On the wealth of elite free people of color in the South in the period 1800–1861 see Loren Schweninger, *Black Property Owners in the South, 1790–1915,* chap. 4. On their social status and their view of themselves see Berlin, *Slaves without Masters,* 273–83. For a brief but illuminating discussion of class in the antebellum black community see Richard L. Bushman, *The Refinement of America—Persons, Houses, Cities,* 434–40.

> When respectable white men and women can sit and listen to the oratorical displays of Fred Douglass and his able compatriots; when the question of Emancipation is taking hold of the minds of the people in our own State and is fast growing to be the leading topic of the day; when our country is threatened with a war with the most powerful nation in Europe on account of difficulties growing out of the slave-trade—in such a state of public affairs, the author deems it not inappropriate to take a cursory glance at society as it exists amongst the free colored people of St. Louis.

In 1858 Cyprian Clamorgan judged the moment right to publish a short account of a world few white people knew anything about. The result was a series of witty and entertaining vignettes linked by a serious message about race, class, and power. Always the opportunist, Cyprian Clamorgan had an eye to potential sales, and he was certainly not averse to publicity. It might even help him and his family in their business. *The Colored Aristocracy of St. Louis* was bound to attract attention in St. Louis itself, and probably elsewhere in Missouri. After all, in 1858 the status of men and women of color was exciting intense debate across the nation, and in few places was that debate as heated as in Clamorgan's native city. The Dred Scott case, decided by the U.S. Supreme Court barely a year before, had had its origins in St. Louis. Proslavery and antislavery forces were contending for political control of Missouri—and would continue to do so in the tumultuous years ahead. Slavery and the rights of free people of color had troubled Missouri since its days as a territory. The time and the place were both right for a work like *The Colored Aristocracy of St. Louis.* Its very title demanded attention and was bound to elicit a response, although the nature of that response would depend on who one was and what one believed. White people might thumb through its pages because they thought it promised amusing, and possibly scurrilous, anecdotes, or because they were outraged at the very notion of a "colored aristocracy" and were eager to read Clamorgan's arguments so they could demolish them. As for free people of color, who among them could resist seeing whether Clamorgan had included them in his "aristocracy," or reading what he had to say about their neighbors? And, with a name like Clamorgan, he was assured of a readership. Who better to comment on "the colored aristocracy of St. Louis" than a man whose family had been a vital part of that aristocracy for decades?

Who was Cyprian Clamorgan? In terms of racial definition, he was a mulatto, a man of color. His mother had been a free woman of color and his father a white man. Clamorgan was the product of an urban environment, a fact that set him apart from the vast majority of Americans, black and white, in a nation that was fundamentally rural. When he attended church (which one suspects was not often), he identified himself as a Catholic. As for his intellectual achievements, one need only glance at his writing to see that he was exceptionally well-read.

Cyprian Clamorgan had been orphaned within days of his birth in 1830. Eventually his white guardian had sent him out of his home state, and away from all that he had known, in order to get him an education. He returned to St. Louis a cultivated and articulate young man, eager to make something of himself and frustrated at the barriers to his advancement. As for his financial standing, he knew he and his half-brothers should have been among the wealthiest people in Missouri, if not in the nation, but questions of race and legitimacy combined with the activities of dishonest attorneys and rapacious white businessmen, and the general inertia of "the system," to cheat them of their inheritance. That rankled with Clamorgan and eventually obsessed him.

In a very real sense, the St. Louis Cyprian Clamorgan grew up in was still struggling with the monumental changes that had come about as a result of the Louisiana Purchase. In 1818, according to future Mayor John F. Darby, a mere third of the city's inhabitants were Anglophone Americans, and "The prevailing language of the white persons on the streets was French." As for the people of color, "the [N]egroes of the town all spoke French. All the inhabitants of the town used French to the [N]egroes." Darby also recalled that the St. Louis of his youth had a reputation as a wild city, full of "ruffians, robbers, swearers, and swindlers."[3]

The economy of St. Louis was volatile during the 1810s and 1820s. The "fever" (probably malaria) for which the frontier town was notorious struck with especial virulence in 1819, 1820, and 1821. The Panic of 1819 brought bank failures, the inevitable result of land speculation and dubious banking practices. Land values dropped sharply and businesses folded. Gradually, though, things began to change. Statehood in 1821 brought in a steady stream of migrants from Virginia and Kentucky. Land sales picked up, and St. Louis also became an important supply center for settlers heading farther west. Trade with Santa Fe brought in wealth. Then the steamboats arrived. St. Louis became an important Mississippi-Ohio port,

3. John F. Darby, *Personal Recollections of Many Prominent People Whom I Have Known, and Events—Especially of Those Relating to the History of St. Louis—During the First Half of the Present Century,* 5.

and, because of the steamboat trade, there were links with other regions of the nation. Even the Indian trade, the key element in the city's prosperity under French and Spanish colonial rule, began to flourish once more.[4] As more migrants came, the French element weakened. The voyageurs and the fur traders were squeezed out. Some of the old French settlers packed up and left. Others accepted what they could not change and made the best of it. After all, the city's newfound prosperity benefited them as much as it did the new English-speaking settlers.

In time, St. Louis became a haven for European immigrants, most of them German, but a fair number from Ireland. The city, like many others, North and South, in the decades before the Civil War, was beset by ethnic and religious animosities that on occasion led to rioting. Like other cities, St. Louis experienced overcrowding, unemployment, and lawlessness. City services were strained to the breaking point. Political turmoil was a fact of life.

St. Louis was a border city. That was true geographically. It was also true economically and politically. In 1858, when Cyprian Clamorgan wrote *The Colored Aristocracy of St. Louis,* the city was grappling with its sense of identity. Was it a western city with ties to the North and a dwindling commitment to the "peculiar institution," or was it a southern metropolis, ready to secede from the Union if things reached that point?[5] Those contradictions, that inner struggle over the city's allegiance, would tear at the fabric of St. Louis's social, political, and economic life when war finally came.

Where did black people fit in this thriving urban center? To begin with, they made up an ever-declining percentage of the city's population, largely because of massive white immigration. In 1850 black people, free and slave, accounted for just 5.21 percent of the city's residents. By 1860 the figure was 2 percent. As for the balance between slaves and free people, that was also changing. The 1850 census recorded 1,398 free blacks and 2,656 slaves in St. Louis County. A decade later there were 1,755 free blacks and 1,542 slaves. Slavery in St. Louis might have been in decline, but it was not dead. The city still functioned as a major slave market.[6]

4. Glen E. Holt, "St. Louis's Transition Decade, 1819–1830," 366–69, 375–77.

5. For a discussion of the economic crises that beset St. Louis in the 1850s, and the link between those crises and its changing image as a "southern" city, see Jeffrey S. Adler, *Yankee Merchants and the Making of the Urban West: The Rise and Fall of Antebellum St. Louis,* chap. 7.

6. Curry, *The Free Black in Urban America,* 246. Lawrence O. Christensen, "Black St. Louis: A Study in Race Relations, 1865–1916," 270. William Hyde and Howard L.

The "colored aristocracy" of St. Louis—its composition, its function, its wealth, its visibility—was shaped by the history of the city and by the continued existence of slavery. Slavery had existed in the Mound City since its founding by the French in 1764. Would it continue? Cyprian Clamorgan hoped it would not. He was not a Garrisonian abolitionist. Indeed, he had harsh words for the militants in the antislavery movement. However, he made no secret of his distaste for slavery, and he expressed himself plainly regarding the extent to which the fate of free people of color in St. Louis was bound up with that of the slaves:

> [T]he wealthy free colored men of St. Louis . . . know that the abolition of slavery in Missouri would remove a stigma from their race, and elevate them in the scale of society . . . When slavery is abolished, where will be found the power of excluding the colored man from an equal participation in the fruits of human progression and mutual development? What political party will then dare to erect a platform on which the black man cannot stand side by side with his white brother?

The problem of what to do about slavery had apparently not greatly troubled the French and Spanish settlers. They enslaved both black people and Native Americans. On occasion, they freed their slaves. A slave might buy his or her freedom. An owner might be motivated by affection for a faithful servant, a slave concubine, or a child he had fathered. Cyprian Clamorgan was well aware of such arrangements. His mother was the daughter of a slave owner and a slave. In 1809, worried that his child might be sold by his creditors after his death, her father had a deed drawn up giving her her freedom.

Slavery in St. Louis under French and Spanish rule was not especially benign, but there were ways for the fortunate or industrious slave to get free of the system. Once free, a man or woman of color could amass property, including slaves. As for enjoying civil rights, that was another matter.[7]

Then came the Louisiana Purchase. The slavery of black people was a highly contentious issue in Missouri even before statehood. The Missouri Compromise removed any doubts about the legality of slavery in the new

---

Conrad, *Encyclopedia of the History of St. Louis,* vol. 4, 2082. Lloyd A. Hunter, "Slavery in St. Louis, 1804–1860," 233–65.

7. On the *Code Noir* and the treatment of slaves and free people of color in French and Spanish St. Louis see Lorenzo J. Greene, Gary B. Kremer, and Antonio F. Holland, *Missouri's Black Heritage,* rev. ed., 13–14.

state. However, it left unresolved such matters as how successful slavery would be in Missouri and how long the "peculiar institution" would last. But a dislike of slavery, a sense that it was not useful to the new state and did not contribute to its prosperity, was not necessarily translated into a willingness to accept black residents of the state as "men and brothers." As Cyprian Clamorgan came of age, most of those whites in Missouri who advocated the abolition of slavery insisted it must be accompanied by the wholesale colonization of black people as far away from Missouri as possible.

Frankly, free people of color were not wanted in Missouri, as politicians, legislators, and white voters made abundantly clear. Laws were passed to try to prevent free black residents of other states from settling in Missouri, or to require them to post a substantial bond and secure a license if they wished to do so. Legislation at the state level was bolstered by local ordinances in St. Louis and other communities. Were such legal restrictions effective? Clearly they were not. Free people continued to arrive, and not all of them acquired licenses.[8] However, several of Clamorgan's "aristocrats" had brushes with the law over the matter of a license. Two of them, Charles Lyons and Robert Jerome Wilkinson, sued, but to no avail. Possibly, they and others like them came to the attention of the authorities because of their wealth, while other poorer migrants went undetected.

The same laws intended to curb the size of the free black population were also designed to limit access to education. After 1847 it was technically illegal to operate a school for black children, free or slave, in Missouri. However, in St. Louis there were those, black and white, who defied the law, including Catholic nuns and priests, and African American Baptist minister John Berry Meachum, who resorted to holding classes on a steamboat on the Mississippi outside Missouri's jurisdiction. A host of other men and women broke the law, organizing small informal classes whenever and wherever they believed they could escape detection.[9]

Like free people of color in many other cities, the men and women of color in St. Louis had their own churches, but there were fewer of

8. Legislation regarding the licensing of free people of color and the restricting of black migration into the state was passed in 1835, 1843, and 1847. Donnie D. Bellamy, "Free Blacks in Antebellum Missouri, 1820–1860," 205; Maximilian Reichard, "Black and White on the Urban Frontier: The St. Louis Community in Transition, 1800–1830," 11, 14, 17; Judy Day and M. James Kedro, "Free Blacks in St. Louis: Antebellum Conditions, Emancipation, and the Postwar Era," 118–19.

9. Bellamy, "Free Blacks in Antebellum Missouri," 223–24. Day and Kedro, "Free Blacks in St. Louis," 122–24; Christensen, "Black St. Louis," 28.

them than in major urban centers in the North, such as Philadelphia and New York, and they were of more recent origin. The 1840–1841 city directory listed two churches, one African Methodist and one African Baptist. By 1859 there were six.[10] However, Cyprian Clamorgan did not count a single African American minister among his "aristocrats." Many well-to-do free people of color, Clamorgan included, were Catholics. They had either been raised Catholics—a very tangible legacy of the city's French and Spanish past—or they were migrants who had married into old "colored" French families and converted. Newcomers who did not intermarry with old St. Louis families were more likely to join a black Baptist or Methodist congregation. As for Clamorgan, it is possible he did not know any of the black ministers well enough to comment on their lives or their accomplishments. However, it is just as likely that he ignored them because they were simply not members of his social circle. After all, his notion of who was an "aristocrat" and who was not was decidedly idiosyncratic.

Cyprian Clamorgan did not join an African American church and apparently he did not belong to any other specifically black community institutions. He certainly did not notice them in *The Colored Aristocracy.* Despite restrictions on the rights of free people to assemble without white supervision, there was a Prince Hall Lodge. However, there was nothing that came close to the complex network of benevolent, educational, and literary societies that contemporaries described as existing among the free people of color in Philadelphia, New York, or Boston.[11]

Clamorgan was far less concerned than African American commentators elsewhere with the number of black moral reform groups in his native city or the achievements of this or that black literary or debating society. It was not community activism or the willingness to take a stand on any particular issue of concern to the black community that epitomized "aristocratic" standing for him. His emphasis was on the making and spending of money. Wealth was the key to aristocratic status, and wealth in the hands of men and women of color, Clamorgan believed, was the best means of bringing about change. But if wealth was the prime qualification for membership of the "aristocracy," it was not the only prerequisite.

10. J. Thomas Scharf, *History of St. Louis and County, from the Earliest Periods to the Present Day, Including Biographical Sketches of Representative Men,* vol. 2, 1682; Christensen, "Black St. Louis," 31.

11. Hyde and Conrad, *History of St. Louis,* vol. 3, 1374.

In his *Sketches of the Higher Classes of Colored Society in Philadelphia,* written seventeen years earlier than *The Colored Aristocracy of St. Louis,* African American author Joseph Willson agonized over the issue of whom to include and whom to omit:

> I have not the foundation of wealth; because the number who may be permitted to come under that denomination are too limited . . . Nor may I erect upon education, nor occupation; as among the higher classes . . . there is no very remarkable difference to be found.

He finally settled on "that portion of colored society whose incomes, from their pursuits or otherwise, (immoralities or criminalities of course excepted,) enables them to maintain the position of house-holders, and their families in comparative ease and comfort."[12] Even then, he confessed himself not entirely satisfied with his definition.

In contrast to Willson, who approached his examination of the African American elite of Philadelphia with the meticulousness of a social scientist, Cyprian Clamorgan did not expend very much effort on defining the "colored aristocracy" of *his* city. He believed one instinctively *knew* who "belonged," who "counted." His understanding of the "aristocracy" was "those who move in a certain circle; who, by means of wealth, education, or natural ability, form a peculiar class." There were lines of social demarcation one crossed at one's peril. For instance, Virginia Berry "was guilty of a *faux pas* last winter, which for the present has thrown her out of society. The colored people of the second class gave a ball which she attended, and was consequently not invited to a subsequent ball of the first class." Who were the members of the "second class"? Clamorgan promised to tell all at a future date. "Our next attempt will be to give a true account of the *second class* of colored people. The number is large, and the developments we shall make will startle many of our white friends. The romantic incidents connected with this subject surpass the wildest dreams of fiction; and the phases of humanity that will be presented will cause some of our philanthropists and philosophers to open their eyes in amazement." Alas, his second book remained unwritten.

Physical appearance mattered to Clamorgan in a way that it did not to Joseph Willson. Complexion and hair texture were important. Clamorgan did not think it essential to be light-skinned in order to be an "aristocrat," but it most certainly helped. Almost all of his brief sketches include a

12. Willson, *Sketches of the Higher Classes,* 23–25.

phrase or two about his subject's appearance. For instance, Robert Smith, although dark-skinned, was a "fine-looking" man. Allen Gunnell had "straight hair." Antoine Labadie was "nearly white, and look[ed] more like a Mexican than anything else." Thomas Gunnell, the arbiter of taste for the St. Louis aristocracy, was "a Count D'Orsey . . . in bronze," who was consulted whenever "a yellow belle is to be serenaded, or a dark-eyed brunette to be captivated." Preston G. Wells, an alleged informer who "led the life of a spy and a dog," was a "tall, pompous black man." His wife, "a tall yellow woman, uneducated; but having good natural sense and a sound judgment, coupled with great industry and perseverance," was "too good for such a fellow." She was "an Emilia coupled with a black Iago." And so on. . . . Clamorgan hinted he had secrets to tell if he chose. "We, who know the history of all the old families of St. Louis, might readily point to the scions of some of our 'first families,' and trace their genealogy back to the swarthy tribes of Congo or Guinea," but "Such . . . is not our present purpose. Our business is with those who have the mark unmistakably fixed upon their brows." This was his position in 1858 when he wrote *The Colored Aristocracy of St. Louis.* In time, though, some of the "aristocrats" of St. Louis, including Clamorgan himself, would cross the racial divide, either temporarily when the need arose, or permanently.[13]

Would Clamorgan have been shocked to learn that the official racial classification of many of his "aristocrats" changed as their wealth diminished or increased? Perhaps he would, or perhaps he was too well aware of the prejudices and the social conventions that prevailed in not only his native city but also much of the nation to have felt any degree of surprise. The fact was that however people of color saw themselves, they were often perceived by the census-taker in terms of their wealth. An African American man who had suffered financial reverses was likely to find himself categorized as "black," while his neighbor, who had done well financially and perhaps acquired real estate, might make the transition in the eyes of white officials from "black" to "mulatto," or possibly even "white." Members of Clamorgan's social circle, and indeed members of his own family, regularly underwent such transformations.

The compilers of censuses and directories were sometimes swayed by an individual's wealth and style of living, but often they were genuinely befuddled when it came to defining a person's race. So many of Clamorgan's

13. For a discussion of the question of "passing" among members of the African American elite in the period after the Civil War, see Gatewood, *Aristocrats of Color,* 175–77, 337–38.

"aristocrats" had white and Indian ancestors. Compounding the difficulty was the fact that a man or woman of color might have the same last name, and sometimes the same first name, as a white person. For instance, there were dozens of Labbadies and Labadies in antebellum St. Louis, some white and some of African as well as European descent. Working out genealogies and trying to decide whether or not this Antoine Labadie or that Marie Labbadie was white or a person of color was a task better not attempted. It was safer to err on the side of caution and class an individual as white unless one could be certain they were not.[14]

Did one have to be morally above reproach to be an "aristocrat"? Clamorgan apparently wanted to have it both ways. One man of color, he insisted, was excluded from "good society" because of rumors about his wife's conduct before her marriage. And that gave Clamorgan the opportunity to argue that free people of color lived by a stricter moral code than many in the white upper classes. However, he was not as squeamish as Joseph Willson in Philadelphia about "immoralities and criminalities." He included Pelagie Foreman (alias Eliza Lacroix or Mary Holland) among the "aristocrats." This resourceful "Delilah" was a highly paid and financially astute courtesan. There were others whose private lives or ways of making money might not stand up to scrutiny. Samuel Mordecai was a professional gambler. Robert J. Wilkinson, George Carey, and William Johnson were womanizers. Robert Smith was doubly damned. He lived with a woman for some years before marrying her, and he made his money by selling liquor. James Williams "live[d] fast—dr[a]nk fast, and dr[o]ve fast horses." Willson would have excluded Marshall Starks from *his* "higher classes" on several counts. He was a duelist and a gambler, and his "coffeehouse" was in reality a saloon. As it was, Cyprian Clamorgan admired those with a knack for making money. The fact that one was wealthy outweighed the means one had used to acquire wealth. Pelagie Foreman, for example, might have practiced a "contraband profession," but she and her daughter still merited inclusion in *his* "aristocracy." However, it is worth noting that Clamorgan applied a sexual double standard. Pelagie Foreman was rich enough to be an aristocrat, but he insisted her notorious past made her, in some respects, an outcast. While criticizing Margaret Beauvais and Pelagie Nash for spreading malicious gossip about one of their neighbors, Clamorgan was quite ready to hint that various women in his "aristocracy" had secrets they were anxious to hide. By contrast, he regarded a passion

14. For a detailed discussion of changing definitions of race see Joel Williamson, *New People: Miscegenation and Mulattoes in the United States.*

for the opposite sex on the part of his male aristocrats as understandable and forgivable.

Cyprian Clamorgan, the grandson of one of the grandees of St. Louis, was prejudiced in favor of "the old families," but he was forced to concede that the "colored aristocracy" was an amalgam of long-term residents and newcomers. The "higher classes of colored society" constantly received new recruits as a result of migration. Waves of migrants arrived in St. Louis in the years after the Louisiana Purchase, as the city grew by leaps and bounds to emerge as "the gateway to the West." Most of the new arrivals were white, but by no means all of them were. Some of the free black settlers did very well in the new setting. One contingent came from Virginia, the state Clamorgan identified as "the mother of Presidents and mullatos" [*sic*]. Others came from Kentucky, South Carolina, Maryland, and Tennessee. Then there were the northerners. Frankly, Clamorgan could have done without them:

> As a general remark it may be said that the colored people who have come here, especially from the free states, bring with them more faults and vices than they find among those who have been reared upon the soil. We . . . assert it as a fact, that but few of the free colored men among us, who have been raised in those States where the laws make all men literally equal, possess the same amount of honesty, virtue and intelligence belonging to those who have always lived among those whom they have been taught to regard as belonging to a superior race.

If there was movement into St. Louis by ambitious free people of color, there was also movement out. Many of Clamorgan's "aristocrats" caught the "California fever." That was hardly surprising. After all, one of the main overland routes to California in the early 1850s began in St. Louis. Some who made the journey west never returned, either dying en route or opting to stay in California. Others, such as Gabriel Helms and Albert and Charlotte White, returned home with their earnings and quickly acquired "aristocratic" status. The gold fields and the mining towns offered high wages to those prepared to take service jobs. A barber or a cook could earn very good money indeed.[15]

Even when gold was not the lure, the free community of color of St. Louis lost people of wealth, talent, and ambition as they left to investigate opportunities elsewhere. They might go in search of a better education for

15. Rudolph M. Lapp, *Blacks in Gold Rush California*, 22.

themselves or their children. They might hope for a better chance to make money or use their skills somewhere else. Clamorgan made his home in New Orleans for some years, and then in Illinois, before returning at last to his native city, while his elder brother, Henry, tried his luck in Wisconsin.

Some members of the "colored" elite considered emigrating. Samuel Mordecai grew increasingly despondent about his and his family's prospects in St. Louis, and despaired of improving those prospects anywhere else in the United States. He sent his eldest daughter, Julia, to school in England and "talk[ed] seriously of taking up his abode in Paris." A widely traveled and well-informed man, according to Clamorgan, he had come to the conclusion that "[i]n France a colored man is more respected than in any other part of the world." Ultimately, though, he stayed in St. Louis.

As a result of movement into the city and movement out, the "higher classes of colored society" in St. Louis were never static. Clamorgan regretted the arrival of the new families, deploring the diluting of the "French" character of the aristocracy that they helped bring about. But love or loathe the newcomers, he could not ignore their presence. If they brought money with them, or displayed a talent for making money, the fastidious Clamorgan might allow them to be considered "aristocrats," even if they would always rank slightly lower in his estimation than the old "colored aristocrats" of St. Louis.

As far as Cyprian Clamorgan was concerned, wealth was the most important qualification for "aristocratic" status, but how could a person of color acquire wealth in St. Louis? They could inherit it. That was the case with the richest of Clamorgan's aristocrats, former slave Pelagie Rutgers, the widow of Louis Rutgers. Louis Rutgers was the son of Dutch merchant Arend Rutgers by one of his slaves. The older Rutgers left his son substantial holdings in real estate. On Louis's death his property passed to Pelagie and their daughter, Antoinette. Pelagie Rutgers understood that the purpose of money was to make more money. She was a shrewd woman of business who bought and sold real estate in and around St. Louis. Sarah Hazlett, another well-to-do widow, lacked Pelagie Rutgers's flair and her working capital, but she managed to invest in such a way as to provide handsomely for herself and her children. Barber and real estate speculator William Johnson, Sr., knew the wisdom of buying low and selling high, as did the Gunnells, the Labadies, and the Charlevilles. And then there were the Clamorgan brothers—Louis, Henry, and Cyprian—who should have been very wealthy indeed as a result of their grandfather's investments, but saw themselves cheated out of their inheritance.

One could inherit money and then invest it, or one could try to get rich by finding a lucrative occupation and working hard, but that was far from easy in St. Louis. The number of occupations open to free people of color was far less than in many northern cities, or in some cities of the lower South, such as Charleston or New Orleans. Some occupations were closed to them by local ordinances. By the early 1850s, for instance, they had been barred from becoming draymen.[16] The refusal on the part of an employer to hire a man of color, or on the part of white men to work with him, could prove far more restrictive than a local ordinance.

Of course, there was always barbering. Many of Clamorgan's "aristocrats" were in what he referred to as "the tonsorial profession." The designation "barber" embraced everyone from the prosperous hairdresser and keeper of a bathhouse, such as Henry and Louis Clamorgan and Elenius Henley, to the much poorer man with his few combs and razors. On one level, barbering was servile. White customers felt comfortable being shaved by a black barber. The proprieties were preserved. The black man was in deferential attendance on the white. African American men who were careful to show they "knew their place" could do very well indeed as barbers. Cyprian Clamorgan could even take a humorous view of his own and his brothers' profession, picturing the garrulous "knight of the razor" who lathered his customer's chin and then talked a mile a minute while his customer was unable to utter a word.

> It will doubtless be observed by the reader, that a majority of our colored aristocracy belong to the tonsorial profession; a mulatto takes to razor and soap as naturally as a young duck to a pool of water . . . they certainly make the best barbers in the world, and were doubtless intended by nature for the art. In its exercise, they take white men by the nose without giving offense, and without causing an effusion of blood.

James Thomas, a friend of Clamorgan's and also a barber, observed that white American men scorned German or Irish barbers. The black owner of a barbershop would have to explain that he had only hired a white immigrant because he was short-handed. He would take care to attend to his regular customers himself, or send one of his black barbers to shave them.[17]

16. Philip S. Foner and Robert L. Lewis, eds., *The Black Worker: A Documentary History from Colonial Times to the Present,* 58–60. Ira Berlin, *Slaves without Masters,* 231.

17. Loren Schweninger, ed., *From Tennessee Slave to St. Louis Entrepreneur: The Autobiography of James Thomas,* 72–86.

Servile though barbering might be, it could be very lucrative. It could be the means to a handsome living, especially if, as in the case of the Clamorgans, one could diversify. At "Clamorgan's" on Fourth and Pine a gentleman could get a bath as well as a shave, and purchase the finest imported soaps and perfumes from Paris. A barber might invest in real estate, as William Johnson did, or he might alternate barbering with gambling, as did Samuel Mordecai. However, the majority of free black barbers were lucky if they could pay the rent and feed their families.

Then there was the river. White residents of the Mound City grew rich on the trade along the Mississippi, and a handful of "colored" residents managed to do so as well. Henry Alexander McGee and several other "aristocrats" were "boat furnishers," supplying food and a range of other items to the stewards of the many steamboats that docked at St. Louis. A number of "aristocrats" found work as stewards. With tips from wealthy passengers and under-the-counter payments from this and that supplier, one could do reasonably well. Cabin boys, firemen, and deckhands could not expect such largesse. They got their pay and nothing more.

Although the law forbade it, free men of color also ran saloons. Technically, no black person could be granted a license to sell liquor, but St. Louis was a thirsty city, and officials looked the other way, perhaps in return for a bribe. Marshall Starks ran a "coffeehouse" that was really a saloon, while Robert Smith never even tried to call his establishment anything other than what it was.

St. Louis was also a city of transients. A number of widows and married couples in the "aristocracy" ran boardinghouses. How respectable were these lodgings? According to Clamorgan, the ones run by Nancy Lyons and Jane Wells were highly reputable, and catered only to genteel persons. That could probably not be said of all four hundred such establishments listed in the city directory in 1859.

Keeping a boardinghouse was one of the few occupations open to women of color in St. Louis. There was also nursing. Mary Aubuchon or Obuchon was a dedicated nurse, according to Clamorgan, and Nancy Lyons had traveled to France as a nurse in the service of a rich white family. One might work as a seamstress, as did several of Clamorgan's female aristocrats. Then there was prostitution, although few women made the financial success of it that Pelagie Foreman did, escaping death from disease or at the hands of a violent customer, and using her earnings to buy her way into the African American elite. (Clamorgan omitted to mention that after she retired she used her wealth to secure a much younger man of color as a husband). The tragic fact was that if St. Louis offered few opportunities to free men of color, it offered even fewer to free black women. Most, if they listed an occupation at all, were washerwomen. Barber Gabriel Helms had "bestowed a world of pains upon [the] education" of his daughter, Theresa, and she was "one of the most fascinating ladies of the city . . . Her mind is equally gifted with her person, and she is the bright star of all social parties." However, in 1858 she was working at one of the few jobs available to her; she was a chambermaid. It was a sad commentary on the plight of women in general, and women of color in particular. Not until after the Civil War, when St. Louis established public schools for black children, would the daughters, and occasionally the widows, of Clamorgan's "colored aristocrats" be able to enter the teaching profession and put to use for the benefit of the community the education they had struggled so hard to acquire.

Assuming a man or woman of color in St. Louis could make money, how could it be invested? One thing is clear from the various censuses and from their wills: unlike their counterparts in Charleston and New Orleans, the "colored aristocrats" of St. Louis did not buy slaves. There was nothing to prevent their doing so. Slave-turned-preacher John Berry Meachum, who died several years before Clamorgan wrote *The Colored Aristocracy,* had purchased slaves and then allowed them to work off their purchase price. But not one of the men and women Clamorgan named in his book owned a slave—at least not at the time he was writing. Perhaps they found the whole notion of chattel slavery morally repugnant. Perhaps, like many white residents of the Mound City, they did not think slaves would bring them a very good return for their money. Whatever the case, they reinvested their capital in their businesses and bought real estate in and around St. Louis and across the river in Illinois. When they needed domestic help, they hired African American or white immigrant servants.

What did their wealth bring the members of Clamorgan's "aristocracy"? It brought them the outward trappings of success—the handsome piano in the Rutgers mansion, Pelagie Foreman's fine carriage, and the like. Within certain limitations, it brought advantages for their children—an education in Philadelphia for the Hazlett daughters, schooling in England for Julia Mordecai. It also brought the occasional well-intended if downright offensive compliment. For example, James Thomas, "a man of mark—one who has seen the world," was a shrewd man of business, and something of an adventurer, having traveled extensively in the United States and even gone filibustering with William Walker in Nicaragua. "Last summer . . . a compliment was paid him by a gentleman occupying the front rank of the statesmen of the West . . . The gentleman remarked to Thomas, that all that prevented him from becoming one of the greatest men of the age was his color." Thomas, a man of tact and common sense, probably responded in an appropriate manner. As he and his fellow "aristocrats" knew all too well, their safety lay in not being seen to challenge the system. As for openly protesting the existence of slavery, the basic denial of civil rights, and the many restrictions, legal and otherwise, that people of color faced, they understood that was better not attempted. Certain events were etched into the folk memory of the people of color of St. Louis. Two decades before Clamorgan wrote *The Colored Aristocracy,* a free black man had been burned to death in the street by a lynch mob. It was far safer to confine oneself to making money, and using the power that money gave to try to effect change. Free people in northern cities could hold meetings, draw up petitions, organize antislavery societies, and publish newspapers. Clamorgan's "aristocrats" knew from bitter experience how they should frame their protests.[18]

How should wealthy men or women of color use their money? Clamorgan was cynical (or perhaps one should say realistic) about human nature. Money was power, and people responded to it accordingly. Clamorgan predated Booker T. Washington in his philosophy of the power of the almighty dollar to bring about a change in the civil and political status of African Americans. As Clamorgan saw it, the role of the aristocracy was first to exist, second to make money, and third to use that money to buy friends for the African American community. He believed that was already happening, and he was eager to show his white readers "in what manner the political influence of the colored man is felt, and how, in every important election, his interest is exerted in behalf of his favorite candidate." The root of influence was money:

> [T]he colored people of St. Louis command several millions of dollars; and every one knows that money, in whose hands soever it may be found, has an influence proportioned to its amount. Now, although our colored friends have no voice in the elections, they are not idle spectators. They know what parties and what individuals are most favorable to their interests, and they are not slow in making friends with those who are able and willing to serve them.

18. Darby, *Personal Recollections,* 237–42. On the activism of the "higher classes of colored society" in Philadelphia, for instance, see Willson, *Sketches of the Higher Classes,* and Julie Winch, *Philadelphia's Black Elite: Activism, Accommodation, and the Struggle for Autonomy, 1787–1848.*

They had thrown their weight behind the "Emancipation Party" for obvious reasons. They understood that their own fate could not be divorced from that of the slaves. "Wealth is power, and there is not a colored man in our midst who would not cheerfully part with his last dollar to effect the elevation of his race. They know who are their friends, and when the opportunity arrives they exhibit their gratitude in a manner most acceptable to the recipient." Clamorgan explained how they were able to exercise power:

> Many of them own houses which are rented to white voters, and others trade extensively with white dealers. It is an easy matter for them to say to their tenants, 'Mr. Blair and Mr. Brown are our friends—vote this ticket or seek another place of abode.' It is no less easy for them to tell the merchant that, unless he votes for certain men, he will lose a large custom; and no one acquainted with human nature will deny that such requests are usually complied with.

His concept of his aristocrats' service to their community explains in large measure the many mentions in *The Colored Aristocracy* of how much money this man or woman had. Other African American commentators, such as Joseph Willson in Philadelphia, would have considered such observations crass and irrelevant.

His stress on wealth in the hands of people of color led Clamorgan to grossly overestimate the value of various estates. A study of her deeds indicates Pelagie Rutgers was very wealthy indeed, although whether she was worth half a million dollars in 1858 is another matter. Pelagie Nash may have been worth $5,000. Sarah Hazlett, the "fascinating 'grass widow,'" probably did not command $70,000. Mary Aubuchon owned half the wealth Clamorgan attributed to her. Professional gambler Samuel Mordecai may have been "good for one hundred thousand dollars when 'flush,'" but in 1860 the census taker put his wealth at less than $15,000. Robert J. Wilkinson had $6,500, not $21,000. And so on. However, Clamorgan estimated Albert White's estate at $15,000, while the census-taker valued it at more than $21,000. Barriteer Hickman was worth considerably more than the $5,600 that, according to Clamorgan, he had put by "for a rainy day." As for the wily former courtesan Pelagie Foreman, she may well have had the $100,000 Clamorgan credits her with having amassed from her "contraband profession."[19] However, whether he was accurate in his

19. Christensen has calculated that free people owned $221,498 in real estate and personal property in the census of 1860 [26]. The figure probably was higher, though,

estimates, or prone to wild exaggerations, it did not blunt the force of his argument. Men and women of color commanded wealth. White people should acknowledge that—and many had already done so. As for aspiring "aristocrats of color," they must amass wealth and use it. They could squander it, or they could invest it to "buy" friends and influence the political process.

Clamorgan looked to a day when slavery would be abolished and men and women judged on nothing more than their merits. Then his aristocrats would come into their own. In fact, very few of the people he wrote about assumed leadership positions in the African American community of St. Louis after the war. There were exceptions. Significantly, Preston G. Wells, against whom Clamorgan leveled some of his most scathing comments, spoke out energetically on the rights of African Americans. Some aristocrats died or left the city. Others passed into the white community. And still others devoted their energies exclusively to the pursuit of wealth, leaving it to newcomers to agitate for political equality. Was it the case that old habits died hard and that Clamorgan's aristocrats had been accustomed for so long to think it safer to amass money than to vociferously demand their rights? Was it that they had simply grown tired in the struggle to keep their heads above water financially? Were they more than willing to give place to a group of younger, more assertive, African American leaders? Or had Cyprian Clamorgan written with a young man's naive optimism, looking to the members of his class to effect overnight sweeping changes that would, in reality, be the work of generations?[20]

What was the response to Cyprian Clamorgan's book? That is a difficult question to answer. He certainly did not grow rich from it, but perhaps he did not expect to. Did it make him persona non grata in St. Louis? Apparently it did not. The proverbial "rolling stone," he traveled a great deal in the years after its publication, but he had left St. Louis for extended trips up and down the Mississippi before. There is nothing to suggest that irate whites, or equally enraged people of color, drove him out. As for his book, it did not sink without a trace, but it was very much an ephemeral work. Loosely bound and printed fairly cheaply, it was not the kind of

---

because a number of Clamorgan's "aristocrats" were listed as white, and several who were substantial property owners, as evidenced by property deeds, were listed by the census-taker as having no property.

20. For discussions of the situation of African Americans in St. Louis after the Civil War see Christensen, "Black St. Louis," and Greene, Kremer, and Holland, *Missouri's Black Heritage*, chap. 7.

thing someone kept as part of their private library and passed on to their heirs. Apparently, hardly anyone thought it was worth preserving. The only surviving copy is in the Missouri Historical Society in St. Louis.

As far as is known, Cyprian Clamorgan never tried his hand at writing anything else for publication. That is a pity. His devastating thumbnail sketches of friend and foe still have the power to amuse as well as inform. As for his serious purpose, to explore the interconnections of race, class, money, and power, that remains as timely today as it was 140 years ago.

The Clamorgans of St. Louis

> When Upper Louisiana was settled by the French and Spaniards, the emigrants were necessarily all of the sterner sex . . . [T]aking up their abode in the wild wilderness, where beasts of prey and prowling savages beset them on all sides, they could not bring with them the soft partners of their bosoms . . . But man without woman . . . becomes a savage, morose and discontented being. He longs for the endearments of a wife, and sighs for the prattle of children in the solitude of his forest home . . . At that time the blood of Africa had crossed the Atlantic, and the colored race had found a foothold in the West Indies. It was there that many of the voyageurs . . . obtained wives to share their fortunes in the wilderness; and from this union have sprung up many of those whom we designate the "colored aristocracy."[1]

Cyprian Clamorgan, the author of *The Colored Aristocracy of St. Louis,* cast a rosy glow over the unions of voyageurs and women of color. True, some of those unions were marked by a deep and abiding affection on both sides, but many more were the result of coercion and the exercise of the power that the law gave a master over his "chattel personal." As for the stability of these interracial families, few of the women were accorded the legal status of wives. When their lovers took white wives, as most did, the women of color were generally relegated to the position of concubines. As for the children, they might remain slaves, bound to their white siblings for life, but some did secure their freedom, and a few amassed wealth, either through bequests from their fathers or through their own industry. In St. Louis, as Cyprian Clamorgan observed, it was those men and women who constituted the backbone of the "colored aristocracy." Prone though he was to romanticizing the harsh realities of life, Clamorgan knew what he

1. Cyprian Clamorgan, *The Colored Aristocracy of St. Louis,* 1.

was writing about. He and his half brothers, who considered themselves integral members of the "colored aristocracy" of St. Louis, were the grandchildren of a voyageur and a woman of color.

Jacques Clamorgan (ca. 1734–1814), Don Yago Clamorgan, Santiago Clamorgan, or James Morgan, went by a host of aliases. As to his character, opinions differed widely. He was either a farsighted man of business or an unmitigated scoundrel, a fearless adventurer or a consummate trickster who would lead to ruin anyone foolish enough to listen to his grandiose schemes. Jacques Clamorgan spent his early years in the French West Indian colony of Guadeloupe. Of his parentage nothing is known. He was, according to various accounts, of mixed Spanish, Portuguese, Scottish, Welsh, French, and perhaps West African extraction. He first surfaced around 1780, trading slaves between Jamaica and New Orleans. His home, insofar as he called anywhere home, was Illinois, although he later moved to St. Louis. His trade links extended from Montreal to Havana, and from Santa Fe to Chihuahua. Persuasive, astute, imaginative in the extreme, Clamorgan always had his sights set on making money. Cattle-ranching, rope-making, fur-trading, lead-mining—over the years there were few enterprises he did not engage in. Fluent in French, Spanish, and the languages of many of the native peoples of the Mississippi Valley and northern Mexico, he ranged the frontiers of New Spain for months at a time, even in old age. He was as much at home in a Pawnee village as in his modest house in St. Louis. Over the years he made and lost several fortunes. There were shady dealings over the Company of the Discoverers and Explorers of the Missouri. Somehow, Clamorgan ended up with almost all the shares in his hands. When creditors—and there were plenty—came after him, they seldom got any satisfaction in the courts. First they had to find him. Then they had to convict him. Finding him involved waiting for him to return from yet another trading venture. And convicting him of fraud or embezzlement was not easy. Plenty of small traders on the frontier owed him money, and they were not about to testify against him.[2]

2. A. P. Nasatir, "Jacques Clamorgan: Colonial Promoter of the Northern Border of New Spain," 104, 105, 106–7, 109. Richard Edward Oglesby, the author of *Manuel Lisa and the Opening of the Missouri Fur Trade,* describes Clamorgan as "a Portuguese of dubious ancestry and background" (p. 17). For a sense of the varied nature of Clamorgan's business activities see Nasatir, ed., *Before Lewis and Clark: Documents Illustrating the History of Missouri, 1785–1804,* vols. 1 and 2; Noel M. Loomis and Abraham P. Nasatir, *Pedro Vial and the Roads to Santa Fe;* Nasatir, *Borderland in Retreat: From Spanish Louisiana to the Far Southwest;* and Oglesby, *Manuel Lisa.*

Adventurers and promoters were hardly out of place in the frontier settlement of St. Louis, but somehow Jacques Clamorgan never quite fit in with the Chouteaus and the Papins, the Laclèdes and the Labbadies. There was his wanderlust and the reputation he had for being none too honest. But most of the self-styled grandees of St. Louis had been involved at one time or another in dubious business transactions. What they found unpalatable about Jacques Clamorgan was his rejection of their lifestyle. Whereas most of them took European or white Creole wives and kept black or Indian women as concubines, Jacques Clamorgan lived exclusively with women of color.

Clamorgan's relations with his "Negro wives," as a contemporary described his mistresses, were tempestuous. If the testimony of his descendants is to be believed, he could be deceitful and physically very brutal, beating, threatening, and tricking the women to get what he wanted, be it sex or money. They were his property. He bought and sold them, used them, cast them aside if and when he chose, sired an unknown number of children, and produced a family that was as quarrelsome and as ambitious as he himself was.

Jacques Clamorgan was in the business of buying and selling slaves in the territory that would become Missouri at least as early as 1784. One of his first acquisitions was Esther. Ichabod Camp and his family had moved from Virginia to Kaskaskia, Illinois, with their slaves, including thirty-one-year-old Esther and her young daughter, Celée. Camp was in debt to Clamorgan, and in 1784 Esther was traded to him in partial settlement of that debt. The following year he purchased her daughter.[3]

Esther became Clamorgan's housekeeper and his mistress. One white visitor observed that she wielded considerable power. "[She] seemed to have the control within the premises when Clamorgan was absent, and very much so when he was at home." After a fashion, she also became Clamorgan's junior business partner. He transferred large amounts of real estate to her in 1793—so he later claimed—to hold for him. (He was involved in some highly dubious speculations and was anxious to hide his assets from potential creditors.) That same year he freed her unconditionally. He also sold Celée to her, with the stipulation that the young woman serve her mother for life.[4]

3. Judith A. Gilbert, "Esther and Her Sisters: Free Women of Color as Property Owners in Colonial St. Louis, 1765–1803," 15. St. Louis County deeds, Book A, p. 209.

4. Gabriel Cerre, quoted in Gilbert, "Esther and Her Sisters," 18. St. Louis County deeds, Book A, p. 209; Book B, pp. 312, 313, 319.

Soon after the land transfers, the relationship between Esther and Clamorgan ended acrimoniously. Was the cause Esther's desire to be truly free, a status she felt she would never really have if she remained with Clamorgan? Was it his womanizing? Was he perhaps beginning to tire of Esther, now in her early forties, and show an interest in Celée? Did the move to separate come from him?[5] Whatever the cause of the separation, Esther proved she could survive on her own and provide for her daughter and her grandchildren.

Esther Morgan, as she sometimes called herself, was a tough, resourceful frontierswoman. She acquired land in and around St. Louis from the Spanish governor and soon had a successful farm. However, as her heirs told the story, Jacques Clamorgan suffered a reversal in his fortunes in 1808, and he demanded that Esther give him her land. She refused. He then beat her, verbally abused her, and finally threatened to sell Celée and her children in the slave market in New Orleans, claiming they were not legally free. Esther was terrified. She was illiterate and, so her grandchildren claimed, Clamorgan took advantage of that, forging documents stating that she had given him her land. She hired a lawyer, who proved as dishonest as Clamorgan. He tried to get her land for himself, and he conspired with Clamorgan. The case dragged on long after the deaths of Jacques, Esther, Celée, and two of Celée's children.[6]

When Jacques Clamorgan freed Esther, he quickly replaced her with other "Negro wives." There was Hélène, who presented him with a son, St. Eutrope, on April 30, 1799. Apoline, born on February 7, 1803, was his daughter by Susanna. Judith Pelissier bore him two more children,

5. Gilbert, "Esther and Her Sisters," 19.

6. Celée had five children: Teresa Denys or Dennis, Agatha Scavener, Joseph Scavener, Francis Fitzgerald, and Edward Fitzgerald. Edward Fitzgerald had been born to Celée while she was still legally Jacques Clamorgan's slave. The child's father was a visiting English nobleman. Clamorgan freed Edward, technically his property, "for one hundred dollars paid him by Lord Edward Howard, reputed father of the boy." Edward Fitzgerald (he sometimes called himself Edward Clamorgan) moved to Kentucky but subsequently returned to St. Louis, where he died, intestate, on March 13, 1821. His estate was administered by Celée. Celée predeceased Esther, who died in 1833. Francis died soon after Esther, intestate and without issue. His claim on Esther's estate went to his brother and sisters. Joseph Scavener was listed as a carpenter in the 1821 St. Louis directory. By 1831 he had moved to New Orleans. He was still living there in the early 1840s. Teresa and Agatha married free men of color (George St. Pierre or Spears and Thomas Butcher) and made their homes in St. Louis. Gilbert, "Esther and Her Sisters," 19. Charles Van Ravenswaay, *St. Louis: An Informal History of the City and Its People, 1764–1865,* 70. St. Louis County deeds, Book F, p. 8; Book E2, p. 356; Book I2, p. 410; Book T2, p. 74; Book Z4, p. 311. "Petition concerning land grant to Esther, free mulatto woman," in Hamilton R. Gamble Papers, MHS.

Cyprian Martial, born in June 1803, and Maximin, born in 1807, when Clamorgan was seventy-three years old.[7]

Jacques Clamorgan knew the risks he was running as a businessman. He had a fortune one minute and was virtually destitute the next. If he died in debt, his creditors might well try to sell his children, since they were legally slaves and hence part of his estate. To prevent that he executed deeds of manumission for each one of them. He also set about transferring property to them. In 1803 he sold much of his real estate in St. Louis and several of his slaves to his friend, Joseph Brazeau, for a nominal amount. That same day Brazeau gave the land and the slaves to Clamorgan's children. When he made his will in October 1814, just a few days before he died, Clamorgan divided his property, such as it was, into five equal shares. Maximin would get two shares (to compensate for the fact that he had been born after the 1803 transfer), and his other "enfants naturels" one apiece. His estate was much encumbered when he died. In total, it was worth less than one thousand dollars. In addition to his personal effects and the cash he had on hand, he had claims to many thousands of acres of land in Missouri and Arkansas, but his heirs would have to fight to have those claims validated. And every year's delay lessened their chances of success.[8]

In 1814 all of Jacques Clamorgan's children were minors and in need of a guardian. Why he did not leave them with their mothers is unclear. They may have died, or he may have sold them. Surprisingly, after all that had passed between them, he entrusted his children to his erstwhile mistress, his sometime business partner and sometime adversary, Esther Morgan![9] Esther proved a faithful guardian, raising Clamorgan's children and not

7. Oscar W. Collet, *Index to St. Louis Cathedral and Carondelet Church Baptisms,* 53. With a West Indian Creole's eye for racial distinctions, Jacques Clamorgan carefully spelled out for the authorities in St. Louis the fact that Hélène and Susanna were both "Négresses," while Judith was "une mulâtresse." St. Louis County deeds, Book B, pp. 367, 368, 370.

8. St. Louis County deeds, Book I, p. 175. Perhaps on instructions from Clamorgan, Brazeau stipulated that none of the children were to alienate the property until the youngest was twenty-five. That provision gave rise to several lawsuits. See *Clamorgan et al. v. Lane,* 9 MO 447 (1845). St. Louis County deeds, Book B, pp. 367, 368, 370. Cyprian Martial and Maximin also received well over half a million arpents of land in 1813. Jean Baptiste Pelissier stated that his sister, Judith, had given him eighteen hundred dollars "a long time before her death," and asked him "to employ the said sum to buy any property whatever for their use and benefit." All the land passed to Cyprian Martial on his brother's death, and he traded away half of it in 1826 to one George French Strother for "professional services." The rest apparently went to young Henry Clamorgan under the terms of Cyprian Martial's will. St. Louis County deeds, Book E, p. 457; Book M, p. 469.

9. Will of Jacques Clamorgan, Clamorgan Papers, MHS. See also SLGS, *St. Louis and St. Louis County, Missouri Probate Records,* vol. 1.

defrauding them of the money she claimed Clamorgan owed her for her land. (She had other property and was far from destitute.)

One by one, Jacques Clamorgan's children tried to carve out a place for themselves in the rapidly growing city of St. Louis. St. Eutrope was in business as a hairdresser in 1821 at 36 North Main when the first city directory was published. He had married a former slave, Pelagie Aiotte or Baptiste, on April 20, 1820, when he was a few days short of his twenty-first birthday and she was seventeen. They had one daughter, Louise, born on June 21, 1821. She did not survive infancy. Then St. Eutrope fell ill. He died intestate in 1824. Elias T. Langham, clerk of the First Bank of Missouri, and possibly one of St. Eutrope's sister's lovers, was appointed his administrator.[10] The widowed Pelagie married Louis Rutgers, the mulatto son of one of the wealthiest white merchants of St. Louis, two years after St. Eutrope's death.

Then eighteen-year-old Maximin began to sicken. He was intestate and without issue when he died on June 7, 1825. Presumably his two shares of Jacques Clamorgan's estate passed to his brother and half sister. Cyprian Martial was scarcely in better physical shape than Maximin. He was an invalid for some months before his death, at age twenty-three, in February 1827. He at least had the foresight to make a will. Having no children of his own, he essentially adopted Apoline's second son. Young Henry Clamorgan inherited the city lot adjoining Apoline's, and the stone house on it. The rest of Cyprian Martial's estate was to be shared equally among all of Apoline's children, while she would receive any payments due him, along with his horse and cart.[11]

Cyprian Martial noted in his will that Henry Clamorgan and his siblings were Apoline's "natural" children. Apoline Clamorgan never married. Young and legally free, in a frontier town where women were at a premium, she set out to make the best of the situation. Over the years she took a series of white lovers. And, like her father before her, she presented her "enfants naturels" for baptism at the Cathedral Church. How many children she had, though, is not easy to determine. Their names changed, perhaps according to the degree of interest their fathers took in them. Cyprian Leon was born on May 8, 1818, when Apoline was fifteen. He may have been a twin, or he may also have gone by the name of his father, Theodore Papin, a French Creole and a scion of the Chouteaus, the "first family"

10. Collet, *Index to Baptisms*, 53. St. Louis County wills, Book A, pp. 183, 223.

11. "Documents relating to the estate of Jacques Clamorgan," Hamilton R. Gamble Papers, MHS. St. Louis County wills, Book A, p. 295.

of colonial St. Louis. On July 2, 1819, Theodore Papin, the fourteen-month-old child of Apoline Clamorgan and Theodore Papin, was buried at St. Louis Cathedral. Then there was Louis Langon, born on July 25, 1820, Apoline's son by August Langon, another French Creole. Irishman Henry Ford fathered Henry Clamorgan alias Ford, born on July 8, 1822. Charles was born on December 10, 1824, and died in infancy. Pelagie Julie, also known as Louise, was born on February 6, 1828. The baptismal records do not list the fathers of Charles or Louise.[12]

Apoline's health deteriorated as her fifth or sixth confinement approached. She made her will on April 11, 1830, leaving her estate to her three surviving children, Louise, Henry, and Louis, and doing her best to secure a share for her unborn child. The boys were to learn a good trade, and Apoline instructed her executor to "provide a suitable place" for Louise, "and bind or otherwise dispose of her at such place to be educated and reared in a decent and becoming matter." On April 27 Apoline gave birth to another son. She named him Cyprian for his dead half brother and his uncle. Apoline Clamorgan died less than a week later. She was twenty-seven years old.[13]

Under the terms of Cyprian Martial's and Apoline's wills, white merchant Charles Collins became the guardian of the young Clamorgans. He did his best for them, looking after their inheritance and trying to give them an education. Louise died at age six in 1834. Collins sent her brothers across the Mississippi to Illinois for their schooling, and eventually took Henry into business with him, teaching him how to draw up documents of various kinds and how to keep accounts. The Clamorgan brothers stayed with Collins until they were old enough to make their own way in the world.[14]

The first to go into business was Louis Langon alias Clamorgan. By 1842 he was running a barbershop on Tenth Street, between Clark and Walnut. There was a brief stint as a grocer, in partnership with William Johnson,

12. Collet, *Index to Baptisms*, 53, 146, 93, 53. Oscar W. Collet, *Index to St. Louis Cathedral and Carondelet Church Burials*, 86. The dates of birth of Apoline's children are also given in *Landes et al. v. Perkins*, 12 MO 151 (1848). These dates are at variance with those in *Clamorgan v. O'Fallon and Lindell*, 10 MO 77 (1846), but the lawyers in that case seem to have confused birth dates with baptismal dates.

13. St. Louis County wills, Book A, p. 454. Collet, *Index to Burials*, 21. *Landes et al. v. Perkins*.

14. *Clamorgan v. O'Fallon and Lindell*. St. Louis County wills, Book A, p. 454. Collins got permission from the courts to sell or lease some of the Clamorgan real estate to support the children during their minority. St. Louis County deeds, Book R, p. 206; Book S, p. 358. *Clamorgan et al. v. Lane*, 9 MO 447 (1845).

another well-to-do free man of color, but apparently that did not pay. By 1845 Louis was back working as a barber. Business was good. In 1847 he and Geoffrey C. Iredell were the proprietors of the "Italian Baths" at 88 Chestnut, an excellent location directly across from the post office.[15]

Henry Ford alias Clamorgan married Harriet Eagleson, daughter of fruiterer William Eagleson and Catherine Fillicit, on May 18, 1842, in a ceremony conducted by a Catholic priest. He tried to earn a living for himself and his wife as a "riverman," but his earnings were meager, and he decided he and Harriet should start afresh elsewhere. They named Louis their attorney to handle their affairs in St. Louis and headed west to the Wisconsin Territory. They settled briefly in Milwaukee, but soon returned to St. Louis. Louis did what he could to help them. In 1847 he offered them a home with himself and his family. (Louis had married Julia Knight on September 17, 1840, and by 1847 they had two children). Eventually, with a growing family to support, Henry forsook the river for the barber's chair. He worked first on his own, and then, in 1850, he entered into a partnership with Louis. Their "Depot of Elegant French and English Perfumeries, Toilet and Fancy Articles, Combs, Brushes, Razors, &c." was soon thriving, and they took into the business young Cyprian, who had already been working as a barber at the fashionable American Hotel. (Cyprian, too, was a married man. He had married Joanna E. Stewart on November 28, 1850, in a civil ceremony.) The three brothers were ambitious. On June 15, 1851, they pooled their resources and took a ten-year lease on "the corner Store and Basement" of a new building at the corner of Fourth and Pine. They intended to transform it into the most luxurious barbershop and bathhouse in the city. The rent was high, but they were confident they could pay it. To help defray the cost they arranged to let out the basement as a "bowling saloon."[16] Their clients would be able to get bathed and shaved, drink a glass or two of whiskey, play a game of bowls, and probably, if they were new to the city, get discreet directions to the more select brothels in St. Louis.

15. St. Louis directories, 1842, 1845, 1847. Louis also began a series of complex real estate deals. He negotiated various loans that enabled him to buy back some town lots that had belonged to his mother and uncle and had been auctioned off to settle unpaid tax bills. St. Louis County deeds, Book N2, pp. 222, 363; Book O2, pp. 28, 100, 124.

16. St. Louis Marriage Licenses, vol. 2, 401, 271. Henry and Harriet were back in St. Louis by 1846. The following year Louis loaned Henry money, perhaps to help him establish himself in business. St. Louis County deeds, Book O3, pp. 264, 294; Book H4, p. 174; Book K4, p. 44; Book M4, p. 483. St. Louis directories, 1847, 1848, 1850. St. Louis Marriage Licenses, vol. 7, 241. St. Louis County deeds, Book Z5, p. 496.

The grandiose schemes of the Clamorgan brothers had to be rethought when Louis, only thirty-one years old, suddenly died. There is no record of the precise date of his death, but, piecing together the evidence from city directories and deeds, it is possible to narrow it down to the latter half of 1851 or the early months of 1852. In 1851 St. Louis experienced a cholera outbreak. If not as devastating as the epidemic of 1849, it still took hundreds of lives, and in the midst of the crisis deaths often went unreported. Perhaps Louis was a cholera victim. In addition to his widow, Julia, Louis left two sons, Leon (born in 1847) and Julius (1849). Both eventually followed the family tradition and became barbers. (Louis and Julia had lost two other children. Louis St. Eutrope died on September 28, 1846, aged three years, five months, and Apoline died on March 21, 1848.) Julius eventually married one Elizabeth Bell, and they had at least one child, Louis Samuel Clamorgan, born February 3, 1873. Leon married Emily Grice on February 26, 1884. He died in 1888, and Emily married again the following year.[17]

Tragedy also struck Henry Clamorgan's family. According to the 1850 census, he and Harriet had three children—Henry, Fanny, and Kate. A fourth child, Louis, was born in 1851. However, at some point around 1854, Henry lost his wife and three eldest children. His wife's sister, Mary Mordecai, and her husband, barber Samuel Mordecai, came to Henry's aid, taking in his one surviving child, Louis.[18]

Henry Clamorgan eventually remarried. He wed Amanda Woodside on March 16, 1859. They had nine children, seven of whom survived infancy. After a devastating personal tragedy, Henry's family and his business flourished. He made a success of the barbershop and baths on Pine Street, taking into partnership several of the "aristocrats of color" his brother Cyprian wrote about, among them Barriteer Hickman and Samuel Mordecai. For more than three decades, "Clamorgan's" was a fixture in downtown St. Louis. In 1871 the *New York Daily Tribune,* in an article on

17. Evidence from Clamorgan family deeds indicates Louis died between mid-June 1851 and mid-February 1852. Plans for the "shaving saloon" at Fourth and Pine were hastily changed. Robert J. Wilkinson, another "aristocrat" and a distant relative, was brought in as a partner. St. Louis County deeds, Book G6, p. 283. St. Louis directories, 1866, 1869–1888. Lois Stanley, George F. Wilson, and Maryellen Wilson, *More Death Records from Missouri Newspapers, 1810–1857,* 20. St. Vincent de Paul, Baptismal Register, 1867–1877, 263; Marriage Register (from 1867), 177, 271. Julia died in 1883. Virginia L. Guinther, "Deaths Reported in the *St. Louis Globe-Democrat,* 1883," 121.

18. U.S. Census (1850), St. Louis, Ward 2, p. 274. For the approximate date of Harriet's death see St. Louis County deeds, Book 155, p. 213. U.S. Census (1860), St. Louis, Ward 4, p. 74.

"The Freedmen of Missouri," reported that "Henry Clamorgan, with his razor and brush, has made $40,000."[19] Henry Clamorgan died in 1883.

Louis Clamorgan, Henry's son by his first marriage, did not follow the family tradition of becoming a barber. Immediately after the Civil War he secured an appointment as a bookkeeper for the ill-fated Freedmen's Savings Bank. Eventually he became a deputy collector at the St. Louis Court House, a post he held for many years. Perhaps because he had spent so little time under his father's roof, he was closer to his Aunt Julia, the elder Louis Clamorgan's widow, and his cousins, Leon and Julius. He lived with them for some time in the early 1880s, and it was probably then that he met Louise McDougal, the daughter of a neighbor, African American hairdresser August McDougal. The two were married on October 2, 1882.[20]

A decision Louis and his wife made around 1900 eventually thrust the Clamorgans into the limelight and created a scandal that struck at the roots of St. Louis society. They decided to "pass." Henry's widow, Amanda, and her children had already done so a decade earlier, shedding the name "Clamorgan," with all of its associations, and becoming simply "Morgan." Cyprian, when he was in town, did the same thing. It was, after all, such a small journey to make, across what he himself had called "that wavering line" that separated light-skinned men and women of color from their white neighbors. Legally the Clamorgans might even have been considered "white," for Missouri used the one-eighth rule to determine racial identity. Louis Clamorgan's grandfather and great-grandfather had been white. His mother's family had been light-skinned. The McDougals were light-skinned. Who would know? The census-takers had often listed

19. St. Louis Marriage Licenses, vol. 9, 366. Amanda Woodside's origins are obscure. She told the census-taker in 1900 that she and her parents had been born in California. She also claimed to have been born in October 1844, which would have made her fourteen when she wed Henry. Twenty years earlier Henry had reported that his wife was a native of Ohio, that her father was German and her mother from Illinois. Amanda may well have been pregnant when she and Henry married. Daughter Amanda (who died young) was eighteen months old when the 1860 census was taken. Their other children were Clara (born February 18, 1860), Peter Howard (born January 9, 1862 and apparently died young), Lilian or Charlotte (born 1865), Henry (born 1866), Thomas (born February 15, 1868), Oliver (born 1872), Josephine (born 1878), and Amanda (born 1880 and named for her dead sister). St. Vincent de Paul, Baptismal Record, 1852–1867, 324, 403; ibid., 1867–1877, 63. U.S. Census (1860), St. Louis, Ward 2, p. 633; (1870), subdiv. 2, 132; (1880), vol. 36, e.d. 155, sheet 17; (1900), vol. 91, e.d. 150, sheet 8. St. Louis directories, 1864–1882. *New York Daily Tribune,* July 6, 1871.

20. St. Louis directories, 1873–1874, 1880–1896, 1898–1911. LDS, International Genealogical Index.

Julia Clamorgan and her sons and Henry and his family as white.[21] In a rigidly segregated society, the rewards for Louis Clamorgan and his family if they could "pass" were immense.

Louis Clamorgan moved his family into a home in the all-white Ellendale section of St. Louis in 1907. His neighbors learned that he was of Spanish descent and that he had an illustrious ancestor, one Don Yago, who had rendered an important service to the King of Spain back when Missouri was part of New Spain. Louis and his wife had eight children, six of whom survived infancy. Chlotilde and Grace attended all-white schools. Estella Clamorgan, or Blanche Morgan, as she preferred to call herself, worked as a stenographer in a downtown office. She was also a leading member of the new Christian Science Church (an all-white institution) in nearby Maplewood. Brother Walter had graduated from the high school as white and worked for an automobile company as a bookkeeper. There were two more Clamorgans, Cora and Maude.[22]

The Clamorgan daughters were exceptionally handsome and had no lack of suitors. Blanche was being courted by two wealthy and well-connected young men from the Christian Science Church, while Cora had caught the eye of John Collins, the son of O. L. Collins, one of Ellenwood's most prominent citizens. And Maude had married a neighbor, Louis E. J. Davis.

There had been gossip when the Davises moved to Ellenwood. Rumors had circulated to the effect that *they* were "passing." They strenuously denied the accusation. They were, they insisted, of Native American descent. Early in 1911 Maude Clamorgan Davis gave birth to a daughter, Laura. One look at the child was enough to convince anyone she was black. The Davises turned on the Clamorgans. The elder Mrs. Davis confessed that she had long suspected the Clamorgans were "passing." Now the word was out.[23]

The press seized upon the story and began investigating. Reporters quickly discovered that Louis Clamorgan was listed as black on the list of employees at the Collector's Office in downtown St. Louis. As for his wife, the McDougal clan was "well known in negro circles." However, it soon

21. St. Louis directories, 1892–1914. Julia Clamorgan and her sons were white in the census of 1870. Henry Clamorgan was white in the 1880 census.

22. *St. Louis Republic,* June 9, 1911. Louis gave his name to the census-taker in 1910 as "Louis C. Morgan." He said his father had been a Spaniard and his mother a native of Pennsylvania. Perhaps Estella chose to call herself "Blanche" to emphasize that she was indeed "white." U.S. Census (1910), St. Louis, e.d. 459, sheet 98.

23. *St. Louis Republic,* June 9, 1911.

emerged that Louis Clamorgan and his family were not the only residents of Ellenwood "passing." Louis Davis worked at the post office annex in downtown St. Louis. "The records in the Post-master's office show that he was appointed as a negro, and is carried on the records as a negro." Brother William was an attendant at the Turkish Baths at the Planter's House Hotel. The other attendants had known for years that he was a man of color. Sister Pocahontas Davis was a teacher at the Dumas School and "was carried on the records of the Board of Education as a negress."[24]

The scandal surrounding the Clamorgans and the Davises soon spread to the Collins family. The Davises rented their home from the Collinses. It was probably while on a visit to the home that eighteen-year-old John B. Collins met Maude Clamorgan Davis's sister, sixteen-year-old Cora. Collins kept his courtship of Cora a secret from his parents and from hers. In August 1910 he persuaded her to elope with him to another county, where they were married by a justice of the peace. After the wedding they returned to their respective homes. They continued to meet secretly, but by December Cora was pregnant and John was forced to tell his parents and the Clamorgans. The Collinses were not pleased—they had hoped their son would do better for himself socially—but they accepted a fait accompli. Collins moved in with the Clamorgans. His and Cora's child, a daughter, was born in May of 1911. They named her Virginia Blanche.

The Collinses were delighted with their little granddaughter until they heard the reports about her cousin. Mr. Collins, Sr., summoned his lawyer. The marriage must be annulled. Interracial marriages were illegal in Missouri. His son had been duped. The Clamorgans should never have allowed the marriage to take place. He conveniently overlooked the fact that the couple had eloped.[25]

The Clamorgans hurriedly packed their belongings and moved. Press comment was not unsympathetic, although it was noticeably kinder to Cora and her "white" child than it was to Maude and her daughter. The annulment cases—Louis Davis decided to try to get his marriage annulled as well—began working their way through the courts.[26]

The court cases focused attention on the most elusive member of the Clamorgan clan, Cora and Maude's great-uncle, Cyprian. The details of

24. Ibid.

25. Ibid.

26. Ibid., June 10, 1911. The "Morgans" were unaffected by the crisis. In 1914 Amanda and her family were still living peacefully as a white family in their home on Chippewa Avenue. St. Louis directory, 1914. *St. Louis Republic,* June 18 and August 17, 1911. For the reflections of W. E. B. Du Bois on the annulment cases see the *Crisis,* August 1911, 144.

his life and the lives of the members of his immediate family are sketchy. His first wife, Joanna, died soon after their marriage, and he married again. By his second wife, Hebe, he had a daughter. Mary Belle Clamorgan was born in New Iberia, Louisiana, in 1856. Father and daughter eventually went their separate ways. At some point Mary Belle married and was widowed. In 1889, as Mary Belle Morgan Bellanger, she married again. She was living in New Bedford, Massachusetts, and working as a seamstress when she met Augustus Smith, a sixty-seven-year-old printer. Smith had been widowed three times before. Mary Belle became his fourth wife. The trail of evidence linking Cyprian, Hebe, and Mary across half a century and half a continent is a fascinating one. In a 1906 petition to Congress seeking recognition of Jacques Clamorgan's land claims, a St. Louis attorney traced his heirs. Noting that Jacques's grandson, Cyprian, was dead by then, he identified as Cyprian's only surviving child Mary Belle, wife of one Augustus Smith of New Bedford, Massachusetts. A search of the Massachusetts marriage records uncovered a marriage certificate with the date and place of birth of Mary Belle, along with the names of her parents.[27]

As for Cyprian himself, he apparently spent very little of his life in St. Louis, although he was a resident of the city in 1858, when he published *The Colored Aristocracy.* He followed the river. He made his living on it as a barber and steward, and he stopped at various points along it—for a few days or a few years. Over the years he traveled up and down the Mississippi, from New Orleans to St. Louis to Illinois. Tracking him from place to place is no easy task, but evidence of his whereabouts surfaces from time to time in deeds and city directories.

Cyprian was in New Orleans during the war, and again in 1873–1874; he was in Calhoun County, Illinois, in 1875, and then in 1878 he was back in St. Louis. He kept afloat financially by selling his claims to various parts of Jacques Clamorgan's vast and ill-defined estate to speculators.[28] His grandfather's land claims obsessed him. He was determined, by whatever means he could devise, to get what he considered was rightfully his. Charles Dickens's fictional law case, *Jarndyce vs. Jarndyce,* pales into insignificance when compared to the litigation arising from the Clamorgan land suits.

27. House Committee on Private Land Claims, *Claims of Heirs of Jacques Clamorgan, House Bill 17888, 61st Congress, 2nd session,* 19. Massachusetts Marriage Records, vol. 397, 167, MSA.

28. St. Louis County deeds, Book 490, p. 354; Book 492, p. 171; Book 531, p. 275; Book 594, p. 363; Book 1158, p. 340; Book 1240, p. 487. He was listed in the St. Louis directory only twice, in 1893 and 1904.

The Clamorgan claims reverberated through the courts for decades before finding their way into the halls of Congress.

In 1796 Jacques Clamorgan supposedly received a huge land grant "in consideration of great and eminent services rendered to the crown of Spain." Clamorgan, according to those who endorsed the claims of his heirs for compensation, was the "precursor [of Lewis and Clark] in peril, but not of renown." He had "explor[ed] the Indian nations as far as the Pacific Ocean." He had kept the tribes of the Upper Louisiana pro-Spanish. The Spanish crown, unable to pay him in cash for his services, had given him land. His grant, more than half a million arpents (roughly half a million acres) some thirty miles to the south of New Madrid, became a hostage to transfers of power, as the Louisiana Territory shifted from Spain to France, and from France to the United States.[29]

As the area was developed and railroads built, the land increased sharply in value. And there were many other claims to tracts in and around St. Louis that Jacques Clamorgan had supposedly acquired over the years. After his death, and while his children and grandchildren were minors, various individuals had helped themselves to his lands. Delays in bringing suit, seizures of land for nonpayment of taxes, lost or unregistered deeds, the actions of dozens of squatters, and the passage of time all conspired, so it was alleged, to cheat Jacques Clamorgan's descendants of their inheritance. Eventually, the Clamorgan heirs, led by Cyprian, demanded the money they claimed was rightfully theirs. Occasionally they were able to interest others in supporting their rights to various pieces of Jacques Clamorgan's estate. In 1852, for instance, they made an agreement with Isaac T. Greene. He would pursue the claim to one tract and pay them six thousand dollars for their rights. When he tried to cheat them, Henry and Cyprian successfully sued him. There were further dealings with an "unprincipled attorney," James K. Mumford, around the time of the Civil War. He allegedly tried to have Cyprian Martial Clamorgan's will set aside and (so it was charged) get all the Clamorgan lands for himself. He sought to

29. R. H. Prince and C. F. DeLauriere, *Petition of Clamorgan's Representatives,* 1, 2, 3, 13–14. See also *Documents, Legislative and Executive, of the Congress of the United States, in Relation to the Public Lands, from the First Session of the First Congress to the First Session of the Twenty-Third Congress* (Washington, D.C.: Duff Green, 1834; rept., Easley, S.C.: Southern Historical Press, 1986), 469, 491–92, 509, 515, 516, 538, 542, 556–57, 559, 580, 581, 588, 599, 601, 603; and *Title Papers of the Clamorgan Grant, of 536,904 Arpens of Alluvial Lands in Missouri and Arkansas,* 3–4. For an overview of the rash of land speculation that followed news of the Louisiana Purchase and the complex legal issues that arose as a result, see Lemont K. Richardson, "Private Land Claims in Missouri," 132–44, 271–86, 387–99.

strengthen his case by charging that Cyprian Clamorgan, in New Orleans at the time, was serving in the Confederate forces![30]

The lawsuits kept coming. In 1874 the Circuit Court of St. Louis heard *Clamorgan vs. The Bellefontaine Railroad Company, and The Baden and St. Louis Railroad Company,* and *Cyprian Clamorgan vs. Fanny Deaver and John Burke.* By 1880 the suit of Henry, Cyprian, Leon, and Julius Clamorgan against the Baden and St. Louis Railroad Company had made its way to the Missouri Supreme Court. The case dragged on, becoming a suit not merely against the railroad company but against the U.S. government. In 1886 the *Cleveland Gazette* noted that the "Clamergans" were "contestants of the Spanish claim for several millions."[31]

There were occasional victories. In 1874 the U.S. Land Office confirmed Jacques Clamorgan's right to one tract of almost 430 acres. As claims were validated, the Clamorgans were able to make money by selling them off. Usually the amounts were modest, a few hundred dollars. After all, the purchasers had to run the risk that they would not be able to eject the sitting tenants. In 1894, though, Cyprian, now Jacques Clamorgan's sole surviving grandchild, sold one claim for ten thousand dollars.[32] It was not as much as he knew his family should have made from their land claims, but it was certainly better than nothing. And there was always the hope that another round in the Clamorgans' legal battle would bring in the hundreds of thousands, or even the millions, that should have been theirs.

Cyprian Clamorgan did not live to see the various court cases settled. In 1900, suffering from "senility," he entered the Alexian Brothers' Hospital

30. St. Louis County deeds, Book C6, p. 624. *Henry Clamorgan et al., Defendants in Error, v. Isaac T. Greene, Plaintiff in Error,* 32 MO 285 (1862). Esther's heirs made similar arrangements with attorneys to try to get adequate payment for the various tracts of land she had owned. See St. Louis County deeds, Book T2, p. 305; Book Z4, p. 311. *Claim of Heirs of Jacques Clamorgan,* 18–19, 20.

31. *Clamorgan, Appellant, v. The Baden and St. Louis Railway Company,* 72 MO 139 (1880). *United States v. Clamorgan,* 101 U.S. Reports 822 (1879). *Cleveland Gazette,* October 23, 1886. As they had done in the past, the Clamorgans launched these lawsuits with the help of an attorney who was to be paid for his services with a half-share of the proceeds. St. Louis County deeds, Book 492, p. 171.

32. In the 1880s the Clamorgans consolidated a total of twenty-nine separate ejectment suits. *H. Clamorgan et al., Plaintiffs in Error, v. D. C. Hornsby et al., Defendants in Error,* 13 MO Appeals (1883); *Clamorgan et al., Plaintiffs in Error, v. Hornsby et al.,* 94 MO 83 (1887). For details of the various land sales see St. Louis County deeds, Book 485, p. 545; Book 490, p. 354; Book 594, p. 363; Book 1240, p. 487. Cyprian Clamorgan's coup probably stemmed from the confirmation of a sale to Jacques Clamorgan of forty arpents of prime real estate. Cyprian got the sale officially recognized in 1891, almost a century after it took place! St. Louis County deeds, Book 1050, p. 266.

in St. Louis. (He told the Brothers that he was a candy-maker by trade and that he had been out of work for six months. He also told them—or the Brothers assumed—that he was white.) He was discharged into the care of friends by year's end and apparently lived out the rest of his life in St. Louis. He was dead by 1906.[33] *His* heirs convinced Richard Bartholdt, the longtime Republican congressman for the city of St. Louis, to get their claims heard in Congress. After all, at the time of the Louisiana Purchase the U.S. government had undertaken to compensate private landowners. Clearly Jacques Clamorgan had been cheated out of what was rightfully his. Restitution should be made to his descendants. On January 12, 1910, more than a century after Jacques Clamorgan had received his land grants, and some four decades after his grandson had begun suing to get for the Clamorgans what he was sure was theirs by right, Congressman Bartholdt introduced House Bill 17888, "A bill for the relief of the heirs of Jacques Clamorgan."[34] The Clamorgans, it seemed, were to get their inheritance at last. However, the bill went down to defeat, and the Clamorgan heirs were obliged to give up the fight.

33. U.S. Census (1900), St. Louis, vol. 91, e.d. 436, sheet 1. Walter B. Stevens Scrapbook, no. 46, MHS. Donna Carl Dahl, the archivist of the Alexian Brothers' Immaculate Conception Province, kindly searched the Patient Registers of the Alexian Brothers' hospital in St. Louis and supplied the information on Clamorgan's hospitalization. He was discharged into the care of Peter J. Doerr, cashier of the Lafayette Bank, perhaps the bank where the proceeds of his various land sales were deposited. The staff at the Bureau of Vital Records in St. Louis have been unable to find a death certificate for either Cyprian Clamorgan or Cyprian Morgan. For the approximate date of his death see *Claim of Heirs of Jacques Clamorgan,* 19.

34. *Congressional Record,* 61st Cong., 2d sess., 570. Bartholdt reintroduced it in the third session as HR 31185 (*Congressional Record,* 61st Cong., 3d sess., 813), but no action had been taken by the end of the session.

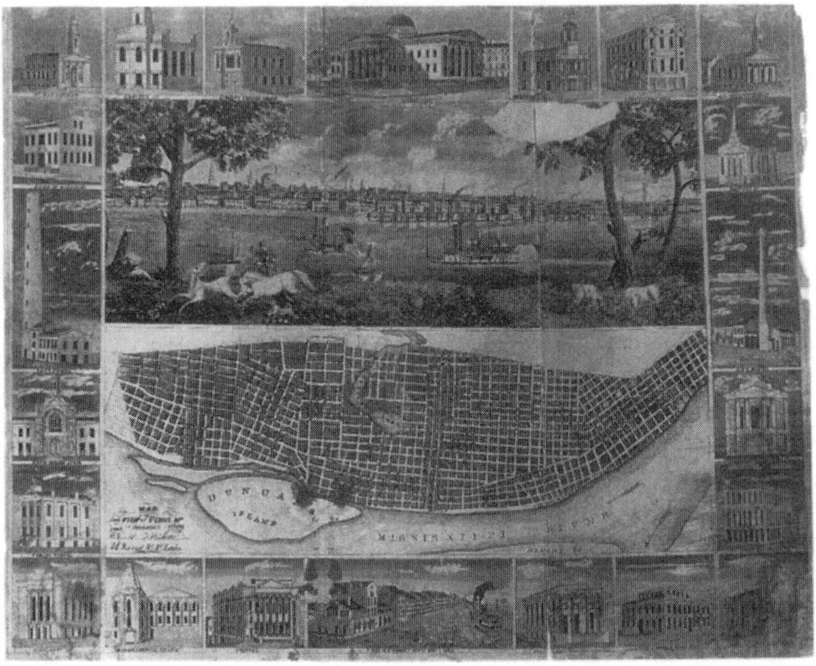

View of St. Louis with vignettes, street map, from *Sloss's St. Louis Directory of 1848.* Missouri Historical Society.

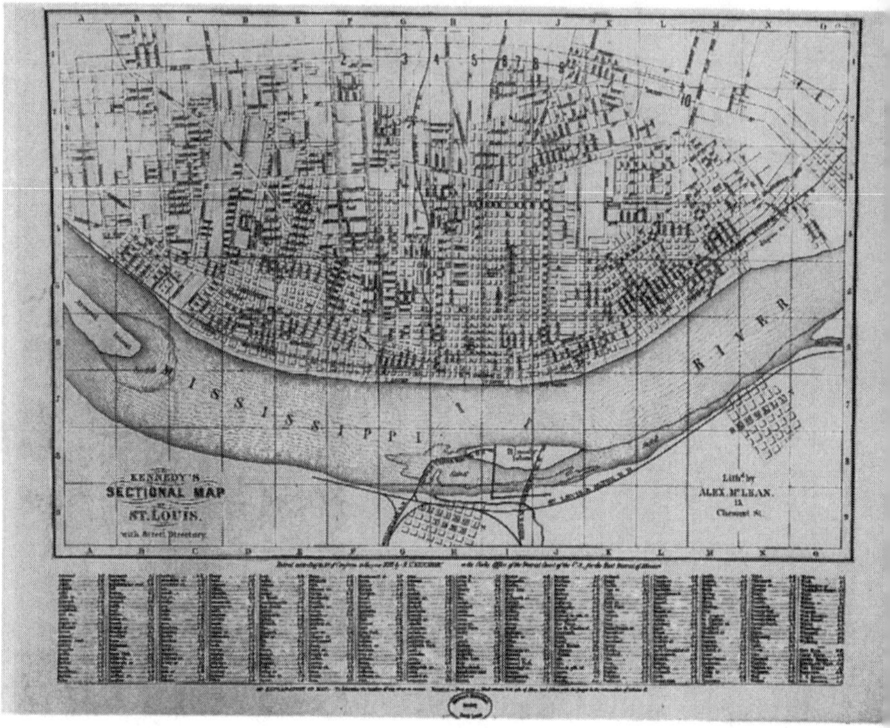

St. Louis, circa 1859. From Kennedy's Sectional Map of St. Louis, lithograph by Alexander McLean. Missouri Historical Society.

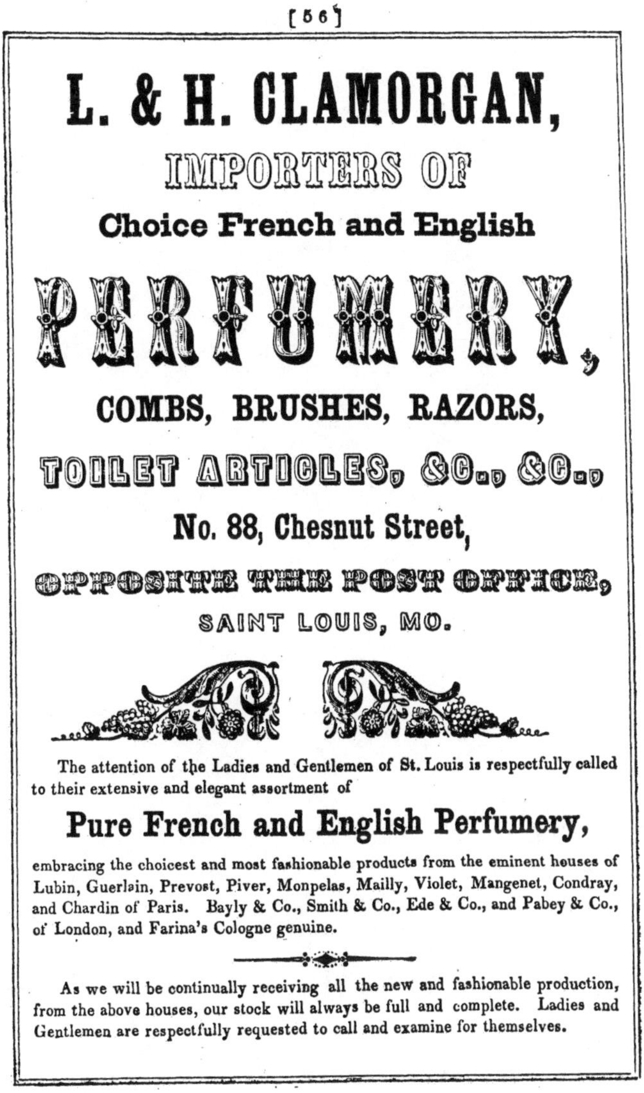

Advertisement for L. and H. Clamorgan, from J. N. Taylor's *St. Louis Merchants, Mechanics and Manufacturers Directory,* 1850. Missouri Historical Society.

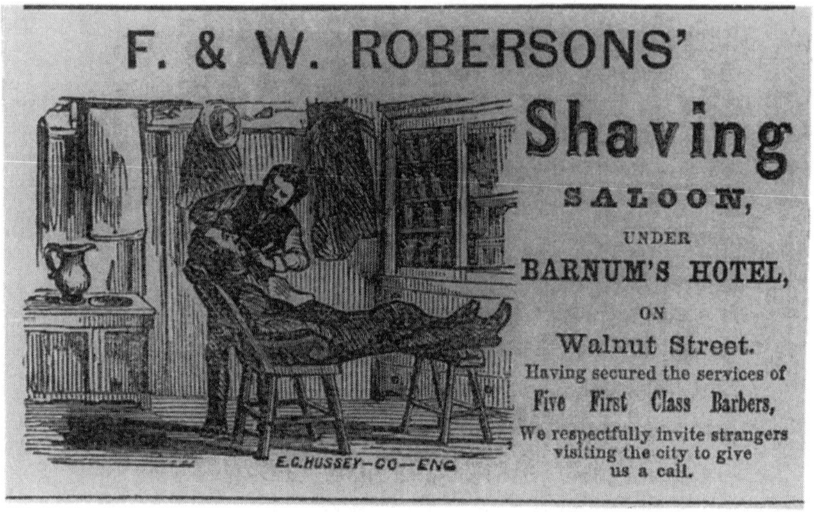

Advertisement for F. and W. Roberson's Shaving Saloon, from *St. Louis City Directory,* 1863. Missouri Historical Society.

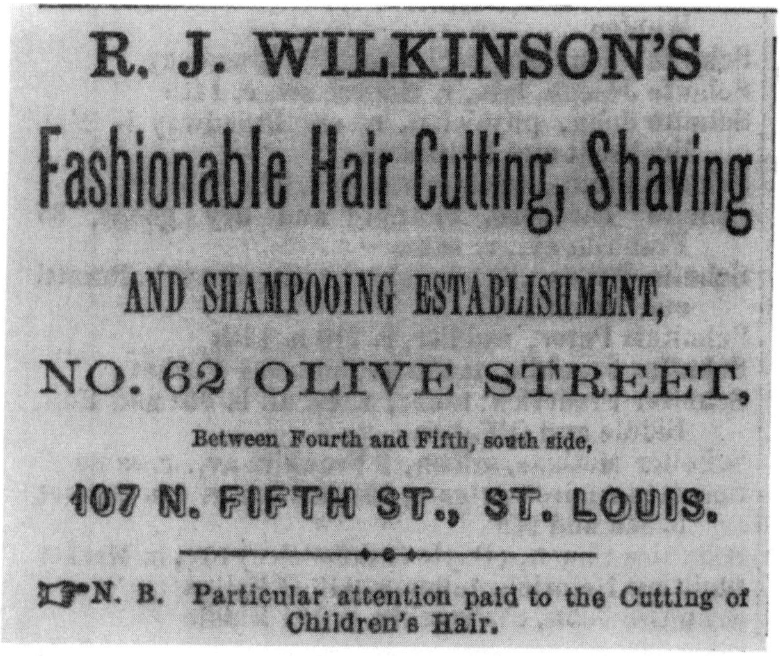

Advertisement for R. J. Wilkinson, from *Kennedy's St. Louis Directory for 1860.* Missouri Historical Society.

Robert J. Wilkinson, owner and operator of the barbershop in the Planter's House Hotel. Daguerrotype by Thomas M. Easterly, c. 1860. Missouri Historical Society.

The Colored Aristocracy of St. Louis

by Cyprian Clamorgan

St. Louis, Mo.

1858

The Colored Aristocracy of St. Louis

Thousands have wept over the fictitious sorrows of "Uncle Tom," as delineated by the facile[1] pen of Mrs. Stowe;[2] while the imaginary "Dred,"[3] a monstrous creation of the same morbid and diseased brain, has awakened the sympathies of all classes of readers. The romantic autobiographies of Solomon Northrup,[4] Box Brown,[5] and other colored gentlemen, have been read in every quarter of the globe. The long-contested suit of Dred Scott[6] excited the attention of the wisest heads in the land, and volumes have been written on both sides of the question. From these and other facts it would appear that the colored race are not without their friends and admirers, even in this land of liberty. When respectable white men and women can sit and listen to the oratorical displays of Fred. Douglass[7] and his able compatriots; when the question of Emancipation is taking hold of the minds of the people in our own State and is fast growing to be the leading topic of the day; when our country is threatened with a war with the most powerful nation of Europe[8] on account of difficulties growing out of the slave-trade—in such a state of public affairs, the author deems it not inappropriate to take a cursory glance at society as it exists amongst the free colored people of St. Louis; to show the origin and position of a portion of those whom circumstances have placed in the path of comparative respectability, and to whom fortune has been kind in the bestowal of the good gifts of life.

The free colored people of St. Louis are surrounded by peculiar circumstances. Many of them are separated from the white race by a line of division so faint that it can be traced only by the keen eye of prejudice—a line so dim indeed that, in many instances that might be named, the stream of African blood has been so diluted by mixture with Caucasian, that the most critical observer cannot detect it. We, who know the history of all the old families of St. Louis, might readily point to the scions of some of our "first families," and trace their genealogy back to the swarthy tribes of Congo or Guinea. Such, however, is not our present purpose. Our business is with those who have the mark unmistakably fixed upon their brows.

When Upper Louisiana[9] was settled by the French and Spaniards, the emigrants were necessarily nearly all of the sterner sex. Stem[m]ing the current of the Father of the Waters[10] in their light canoes and pirogues,[11] and taking up their abode in the wild wilderness, where beasts of prey and prowling savages beset them on all sides, they could not bring with them the soft partners of their bosoms, but left their families in peaceful security at home, while they undertook the task of exploring a continent. But man without woman, even in the wildest state of society, becomes a savage, morose and discontented being. He longs for the endearments of a wife, and sighs for the prattle of children in the solitude of his forest home, and is never contented until he reposes his fevered brow upon the soft bosom of some beloved one whose very frailty is her greatest strength. History tells us that the founders of Rome, feeling the want of a sufficient number of women in their infant colony, seized upon the women of the Sabines;[12] and it may well be said, that warriors fighting in such a cause are invincible. So it was with the early settlers of Louisiana. Having few women of their own, they sought wives among the sylvan maids of the forest; and if the blood of Pocahontus[13] [*sic*] has ennobled many of the best families of Virginia, why may not the descendants of many of the early settlers of Missouri boast of a similar genealogy?

But it was not alone amongst the squaws that our progenitors found companions for their solitude and mothers for their children. At that time the blood of Africa had crossed the Atlantic, and the colored race had found a foothold in the West Indies. It was there that many of the voyageurs[14] up the Mississippi obtained wives to share their fortunes in the wilderness; and from this union have sprung up many of those whom we designate the "colored aristocracy." By this term is meant those who move in a certain circle; who, by means of wealth, education, or natural ability, form a peculiar class—the elite of the colored race. The sketches here presented are mere outlines—facts briefly stated without entering into details. A large volume might be compiled from facts in the possession of the writer, and material for a dozen such volumes as "Uncle Tom's Cabin"[15] might be gleaned from the history of these families, but we only aim at the simple truth, and shall leave all flights of fancy to such romancists [sic] as Mrs. Stowe and her colleagues.

According to the decision of Chief Justice Taney, a colored man is not a citizen of the United States, and consequently has no political rights under the Constitution. His life is all that he is entitled to, and in some States he holds that merely because he is useful to his master. We shall not, in this place, call in question the judgment of the learned Chief Justice, who has in this State kindred of a darker hue than himself;[16] but we may be permitted to show in what manner the political influence of the colored man is felt, and how, in every important election, his interest is exerted in behalf of his favorite candidate.

It will be seen by the following pages that the colored people of St. Louis command several millions of dollars; and every one knows that money, in whose hands soever it may be found, has an influence proportioned to its amount. Now, although our colored friends have no voice in the elections, they are not idle spectators. They know what parties and what individuals are most favorable to their interests, and they are not slow in making friends with those who are able and willing to serve them. Certain shallow-minded politicians among us assert that the so called Emancipation party[17] which has sprung up in our midst within a few years past, is the work of office-seeking demagogues, whose object is to rally the masses of laboring men to their standard by the cry of "free labor." But we assert that the rise of that party is the result of the unwearied and combined action of the wealthy free colored men of St. Louis, who know that the abolition of slavery in Missouri would remove a stigma from their race, and elevate them in the scale of society. The cry has been raised—"Missouri for white men." That is but the entering wedge of human equality. When slavery is abolished, where will be found the power of excluding the colored man from an equal participation in the fruits of human progression and mutual development? What political party will then dare to erect a platform on which the black man cannot stand side by side with his white brother? It is a very wrong idea to suppose that the present movement is designed exclusively for the benefit of the white laborer. Time will show that such is not the case, and we advise the colored man to "bide his time."

I will endeavor to show, in a few words, in what manner the political influence of the colored man is felt in St. Louis. Wealth is power, and there is not a colored man in our midst who would not cheerfully part with his last dollar to effect the elevation of his race. They know who are their friends, and when the opportunity arrives they exhibit their gratitude in a manner most acceptable to the recipient. Among our most prominent citizens who have been the steadfast friends of the colored man, none stands higher in his estimation than John How.[18] He can always depend upon them, in any emergency. He can offer himself for any office in the gift of the people with the certainty of success. Until recently, John M. Wimer might have done the same; but owing to certain acts of his administration he has lost their confidence. Had he been true to the trust they reposed in him, he would not now be in the deplorable position he occupies.[19] B. Gratz Brown[20] is another favorite of the colored men: and should he meet with any reverse of fortune, they would promptly step to his rescue. The same may be said of Frank Blair.[21] Henry T. Blow, also, stands high in their estimation, and may rely upon them for a powerful support in the August election. Mr. Blow was, until recently, a member of the American party; and we shall not reveal the influences that were brought to bear to induce him to unite his political fortunes with the party of freedom.[22]

The colored men of St. Louis have no votes themselves, but they control a large number of votes at every election. Many of them own houses which are rented to white voters, and others trade extensively with white dealers. It is an easy matter for them to say to their tenants, "Mr. Blair and Mr. Brown are our friends—vote this ticket or seek another place of abode." It is no less easy for them to tell the merchant that, unless he votes for certain men, he will lose a large custom; and no one acquainted with human nature will deny that such requests are usually complied with.

A great deal more might be said upon this head; but we leave politics and proceed to persons.

If the reader will accompany me down Seventh street to the vicinity of Rutgers, I will show him a large mansion, which, with the yard and out-buildings, occupies half a block of ground. Entering this mansion, I will introduce him to its mistress,

MRS. PELAGIE RUTGERS,[23]

A brown-skinned, straight-haired woman of about fifty years of age; she is large, fine-looking and healthy, and has been quite handsome; she is worth half a million dollars. Her husband was Louis Rutgers, a free man of color, who inherited the property from his father, a white man of the same name. They settled in the present locality in 1825, and the widow has remained there ever since.[24] Previous to her marriage she was a slave, and purchased herself for the sum of three dollars. About the year 1842 she gave birth to a daughter, and finding that her property was becoming valuable, she requested Louis Clamorgan to act as her child's guardian and to manage her estate.[25] About this time her husband was arrested and thrown into prison, and came near losing all his property. Clamorgan procured his release, paid his debts, secured his property, and he had no further difficulty. I regret to say that for his many acts of kindness, Clamorgan received no reward. At his death the estate was indebted to him in the sum of ten thousand dollars, not a cent of which has been or ever will be paid. Mrs. Rutgers is an illiterate woman, but lives in good style; she has in her house a piano which cost two thousand dollars, but her wealthy daughter, the sole heiress to her large estate, is not able to play upon it. Mrs. R. is a member of the Catholic church, but is not noted for her piety; she worships the almighty dollar more than Almighty God. She makes a fine appearance in society, but exposes her ignorance when she attempts to converse.

Her daughter is an amiable girl, but her mother is too penurious to give her an education. This young lady—the greatest "match" among the colored aristocracy—has bestowed her affections upon a worthy young man, but the ambitious mother wants to marry her to another; so it seems that the course of true love does not run smooth, even among the colored population of our city.[26]

Turning up the street, we come to Third street, between Lombard and Hazel, to the residence of

MRS. PELAGIE NASH[27]

Who is about thirty-eight years of age, and has been twice married. Her estate is worth five thousand dollars; she owns nearly the whole block in which she resides. Her second husband was named Moran,[28] but she is better known by the name of the first. She is very aristocratic in her bearing, and takes great pride in her wealth—her motto being, "Wealth makes the man, the want of it the fellow."[29] Mrs. Nash is very fond of her children, and thinks them a little better than the generality of picaninnies [sic]; her great ambition is to have her daughter marry a man as nearly white as possible; she is rather exclusive in her associates, and evidently looks down upon those who do not possess as great an amount of wealth as herself.

Next door to Mrs. Nash, resides

MRS. SARAH HAZLETT,[30]

A fascinating "grass widow,"[31] upon whose features time has left the trace of beauty, though fast falling into the "sere and yellow;"[32] she is about thirty-five years of age, and possesses a comfortable fortune of seventy thousand dollars. A mystery hangs over the gay widow, which curious eyes have in vain endeavored to penetrate.

Be that as it may, the lady has thus far been shrewd enough to keep her own secret, and to effectually conceal all proofs of criminality between the parties. She is a small active body, quick in her movements, and possessed of great tact in conversation—a talent for which women are generally more noted than men. Mrs. Hazlett is the mother of two interesting and beautiful daughters: Theodosia, the elder, is the colored belle of St. Louis; she is "sweet sixteen," and a marigold of beauty; she has it in her power to choose a husband from amongst the best of her class, and but for the prejudice of caste in this country, many a white man would be found sighing at her feet; her form is the perfection of youthful grace, and her dark lustrous eyes would shame the orbs of the wild gazelle. In short,

"She is a thing of life and light,
Of cloudless climes and starry skies;
And all that's best of dark and bright
Meet in her aspect and her eyes."[33]

Emily, the younger daughter, is about fourteen, and promises to equal if not surpass her sister in those charms which enslave the hearts of men. The girls are both in school at Philadelphia; and, by the way, the Quaker city possesses the best academies for the education of children of color—equal perhaps to the first-class schools of the white race: the teachers are white, and take peculiar pains in their vocation.[34]

We will now turn to the southern part of the city, where, on Soulard avenue we meet with

MRS. MARY OBUCHON,[35]

A widow of forty, though not exactly "fair and fat."[36] She owns the property upon which she resides, and is worth about nine thousand dollars. Mrs. Obuchon has been very useful in times past as a sick nurse, and is one of the best of her profession. She has poured balm into the wounds of many afflicted strangers, and has raised many a stricken form from the bed of sickness. The qualities of a sick nurse are patience, gentleness and watchfulness, all of which Mrs. O. possesses in a high degree. She is a plain, unpretending woman, living in retirement, and does not seek to make any great display in the world. Her daughter Margaret[37] lives with her, and has the general management of the household affairs; she is about twenty years of age, and is a capital housekeeper—one who delights in keeping everything in its place, and has a great antipathy to dust, dirt and cobwebs; she would make an excellent wife, as she has a good disposition, is neat and orderly, and warm in her affections. Both mother and daughter are kind and hospitable, and treat their friends and visitors in the best manner.

Taking leave for the present of the fairer portion of creation, we proceed to take a glance at the "gentlemen of color." On Eighth street, near Rutgers, we come to the house of

SAMUEL MORDECAI.[38]

Although his name indicates a Jewish origin, we are not aware that Sam has any aversion to pork, or would hesitate to sit down to a game of "poker" on Saturday. He is one of the wealthiest of our colored aristocracy, and is good for one hundred thousand dollars when "flush." He is an ardent votary of the blind goddess,[39] and has been one of her prime favorites; he made the greater portion of his fortune by the turn of cards, and is the most inveterate gambler we have ever met with. He has an incurable passion for games of chance, and will bet his pile on anything that has the appearance of uncertainty. From the simple trick of the thimble-rigger[40] or Mexican puzzle[41] to a horse race or Presidential election, Mordecai is always "in." He lives at his ease, but is interested in business at the corner of Fourth and Pine streets. For many years he was a steward on the river, and is one of the most energetic business men to be met with anywhere. Mordecai is a Kentuckian by birth, and has inherited many of the good qualities of the sons of that noble State; he is extremely polite in his intercourse with his equals and inferiors, and quite aristocratic in his feelings. He came here about sixteen years ago, and has prospered ever since. He has an interesting daughter,[42] fifteen years of age, who is at school in England. He is a man of general information, and has traveled a great deal; he talks seriously of taking up his abode in Paris, on the completion of his daughter's education. In France a colored man is more respected than in any other part of the world; some of the most talented men in that country can trace their origin to the shores of Africa, and their blood is no reproach to them. The great novelist Dumas[43] is known to be of African descent, and he makes no concealment of the fact. In Paris Mordecai would be received into the first circles, and has the ability and address to maintain his position in any society in which he may be thrown. He is strictly honest, and his word is as good as his bond.

Reader, if your beard has grown perceptibly while perusing these pages, you will do well to follow us a little further. We will step into the bathhouse and dressing saloon on the corner of Fourth and Pine, formerly known as Clamorgan's, and, after taking a bath and a shave, we will sit down and have a private chat with the proprietor,

ALBERT WHITE,[44]

Who is one of the most expert chin scrapers in the city. He came to St. Louis some sixteen years ago, and has amassed a fortune of fifteen thousand dollars; he is, however, indebted to his excellent and thrifty wife[45] for his prosperity, for when the California fever was raging some years ago, he took her with him to that land of gold, where, by her industry she accumulated a comfortable pile of the dust, which enabled him to return and commence business again. He is a great talker—the common failing with barbers, who are a privileged class. When one of these gossiping knights of the razor gets a customer under his hands, it would seem that his tongue keeps pace with his razor; they are dumb as mutes until they get a man's head thrown back on a level with his breast, his face, and especially his mouth, besmeared with a thick coating of lather, and the glittering steel flourishing in *terrorem* over his throat, and then they shower upon him a perfect Niagara of words. Like a prisoner chained to the stake, he is compelled to listen to the "sentiments" of his tormenter; for if he dares to open his mouth to give utterance to a dry "yes," or a surly "no," down his throat rushes a torrent of lather, that entirely stifles his speech, and chokes him off as effectually as a party nomination gags a small beer[46] politician. I have often thought that barbers were the only men in the community who enjoyed, at all times, the privilege of free speech. Happily, women have no beards, and can talk at all times—but to our mutton. Albert White lives on Fifteenth street near Clark avenue. His education is limited, but he has very good common sense; he is fond of a game of cards, and at times bets pretty freely; at home he is hospitable and kind, and lives well; he is doing a fine business, clearing about three hundred dollars a month; his establishment is the most extensive in the city, and his baths are much frequented.

It will doubtless be observed by the reader, that a majority of our colored aristocracy belong to the tonsorial profession; a mulatto takes to razor and soap as naturally as a young duck to a pool of water, or a strapped[47] Frenchman to dancing; they certainly make the best barbers in the world, and were doubtless intended by nature for the art. In its exercise, they take white men by the nose without giving offense, and without causing an effusion of blood.

Every one who has shaved long in St. Louis must know

BYERTERE HICKMAN[48]

Whose shop is on Fourth street, under the Planter's House. Unlike Albert White, he does not talk much to his customers—is rather quiet, and not a braggadocio, like the majority of his brethren. He tweaks a man's nose with a dainty finger, as though he regretted being compelled to take hold of the human face by the natural handle, and peels off the beard like a dairy-maid skimming cream. Hickman is a descendant of "one of the first families of Virginia," and has been here about fifteen years. He has attended faithfully to his business, and won many friends, besides laying up some five thousand six hundred dollars in cash for a rainy day. He commenced with a small shop on Chestnut street, and was always a favorite with the old residenters [sic]. He has taken the "Moral Editor"[49] through many a hard *scrape*, and the old gentleman is never in a better humor than when he has just come, with a clean face, from the hands of Hickman. His wife[50] is a most excellent lady, and belongs to one of the wealthiest families of Virginia. At home the Hickmans are kind and hospitable, and have many friends in the city.

R. J. WILKINSON,[51]

Another dealer in steel and soap, came to St. Louis sixteen years ago, from Cincinnati. He opened a small shop on Vine street, where a majority of his customers were rivermen. Although indebted to steamboatmen for his start in life, he has frequently taken occasion to slander that noble class of men, whose good qualities are too well known to require any eulogy in this place. The cause of Wilkinson leaving Cincinnati was the seduction of an interesting girl, whose friends swore vengeance against her destroyer. He afterwards married a native of St. Louis, whose connections enabled him to obtain admission into society, and his "youthful indiscretions" have been regarded with a forgiving eye. He has a fine establishment on Olive street, between Fourth and Fifth, and is doing a good business; his estate is worth about twenty-one thousand dollars. He resides on Clark avenue, near Fifteenth street. I am sorry to say his character is not such a one as should be recommended to the young as a model of excellence. He is ungrateful for favors past, and speaks disrespectfully of those who have long been his best friends. He employs good workmen, and his shop is one of the most frequented in the city.

E. HENLEY,[52]

Another of the Virginia bloods, has a shop on Vine street, and is a pattern of a business man. His upright deportment and business qualifications attracted the attention of Ex-Mayor How, who assisted him (as he has aided many men of both colors), and he is now doing well. He can raise two thousand five hundred dollars of his own; and his credit is good for a much larger sum. Henley has a good education, and is altogether a man of sound sense. He has an interesting family, residing on Sixth street, near Cerre. Much could be said in his praise, but his conduct is his best eulogy.

RICHARD MERRIN,[53]

A journeyman in the employ of Henley, is a universal favorite. In appearance he resembles a Moor, and, like Othello, is well calculated to win the heart of the fairest Desdemona[54] in the land. A free-hearted bachelor, he has many friends among the ladies, and is consulted by them on all important occasions—such as the ordering of a wedding supper, the management of a ball, or the christening of an infant. Dick must have a hand in every pleasure party and picnic; and without his presence no wedding would be complete. He is from Virginia, and has been here about eleven years.

MRS. NANCY LYONS.[55]

This lady, the widow of the late Charles Lyons,[56] keeps an aristocratic boarding house, on Sixth street, near Gratiot. Her husband died in California, leaving her the mistress of a fortune of twenty-five thousand dollars, most of which was accumulated by herself. She was born in St. Louis and raised in Cahokia.[57] Living among the French inhabitants she, of course, learned their language, and was educated in the tenets of the Catholic church. In appearance she resembles an Indian, and may possibly have the blood of Pontiac[58] in her veins. She is very industrious in her habits, and pays strict attention to the comfort of the inmates of her house. Her connections are highly respectable, and she has a large circle of warm and devoted friends, and is every way worthy of the high position she occupies.

P. G. WELLS.[59]

As a faithful historian, it is our unpleasant duty to speak of the vile and unworthy, as well as the good and virtuous; nothing but this sense of duty could induce us to mention in this connection a character so far below the common level of humanity as P. G. Wells. He has been here about twenty years, and in all that time has led the life of a spy and a dog. At one time he earned a precarious liv[e]lihood as an informer against his own race. He is a tall, pompous black man—a great braggart, and says more in one minute than he will stand to in a week. He is not only treacherous and deceitful to his own color, but has deceived and cheated every white man who has trusted in his promises. His wife[60] is too good for such a fellow, and supports him by keeping a fashionable boarding house on Elm street. This lady is a tall yellow woman, uneducated; but having good natural sense and a sound judgment, coupled with great industry and perseverance, she maintains a respectable position, and is highly esteemed by all who know her. She is the soul of hospitality and kindness, and takes great pleasure in seeing those around her comfortable. She is an Emilia coupled with a black Iago.[61]

MR. AND MRS. SAWYER.[62]

Of all the colored people of St. Louis, none are more esteemed than Mr. and Mrs. Sawyer. They board at Well's, and are the favorites of an extensive circle of friends. Sawyer is an industrious, hard-working man, and has many estimable traits of character. Mrs. Sawyer is one of the most fascinating ladies of the city; her form is the perfection of womanly loveliness, and would serve as a model for a Venus or an Eve; she is fond of society, gay and sparkling, while her lively sallies of wit spread cheerfulness around her, and her beauty, like a summer flower, awakes the liveliest admiration. Her mind is equally gifted with her person, and she is the bright star of all social parties. Her father, Gabriel Helms, bestowed a world of pains upon her education, and has the satisfaction of seeing his labors amply rewarded in his accomplished daughter, who is the pride and solace of his declining years.

WILLIAM JOHNSON, SR.[63]

If we should search for an example of clear foresight and shrewdness in business, we could not find one possessed of these qualities in a more eminent degree than William Johnson. In 1840 he opened a barber's shop on Main street, with a slender capital, and, in a few years, by close attention to business and the exercise of economy, he saved a thousand dollars. At that time real estate in St. Louis was worth much less than at present, for the city had but commenced to expand with that rapidity which has been one of the marvels of the day. Johnson saw the swelling of the tide in the distance, and determined to take advantage of his knowledge. With the sum he had saved, he purchased a block on Market street, which in a short time he sold for one hundred thousand dollars. Not so bad a speculation for a colored man! He resides on Poplar street, where he has a fine brick house and owns about half the block. His estate is valued at one hundred twenty-five thousand dollars. He has a large family, and several accomplished and highly educated daughters. He is rather reserved in his intercourse with society, a trifle too haughty in his bearing, and excessively proud of his family; he is a good neighbor, however, and is kind and hospitable at home. Johnson's greatest fault is his fondness for the gentler sex—the flashing eye and silvery voice of a golden-cheeked beauty, can raise a commotion in his breast almost equal to an eruption of Vesuvius; it is a fault, however, which men censure lightly, and women are apt to forgive.

WILLIAM JOHNSON, JR.[64]

A nephew of the last named, keeps a coffee-house for colored people on the corner of Washington avenue and Seventh street. He is something of a talker, and pretends to know a great deal; like his uncle, he is proud and aristocratic, but a good business man; he has made some ten thousand dollars, and is very fond of money; he has an accomplished wife, and is in good standing in society.

ANTOINE LABADIE[65]

Is now about forty years of age, and is one of the wealthiest colored men in the city. His estate is valued at three hundred thousand dollars. He is a butcher by trade, and has done a heavy business in shipping cattle to the Southern markets. Labadie is nearly white, and looks more like a Mexican than anything else; he is plain and unostentatious in his dress and manners, and has few of the prejudices common to his class; he was born and raised in St. Louis, and resides at the corner of Clark avenue and Fifteenth street; he is kind and hospitable and of a friendly disposition.

PETER LABADIE,[66]

A brother of Louis, lives in Illinois, on a farm, but owns considerable property in the city. He is worth about twenty-five thousand dollars. His character is similar to that of his brother. He leads a quiet, contented life, and is not disturbed by the jars and discords of the world; but, like a true philosopher, pursues the even tenor of his way, delighting in the pursuits of agriculture and the beauties of nature.

LOUIS CHARLEVILLE,[67]

Who is well known to all our business men, is a large cattle dealer, and ships great numbers of beeves every year. He was once very wealthy, but his estate has now dwindled down to about sixty thousand dollars. He is a shrewd business man, and has a hungry, care-worn appearance. Charleville was born and raised here, and is a strict member of the Catholic church. When he was broken up in business, the Bishop[68] came to his assistance and set him up again. His residence is on Clark avenue, between Fifteenth and Sixteenth streets. His great ambition is to marry one of his sons to the wealthy daughter of Mrs. Rutgers, but the young lady does not appear to smile upon his suit; the courtship is like the wooing of Mistress Ann Page by Master Slender—the old man doing most of the "soft talk" himself.[69]

MR. AND MRS. COX.[70]

Of all the colored men from abroad, Cox is, without doubt, the best. As a general remark it may be said that the colored people who have come here, especially from the free States, bring with them more faults and vices than they find among those who have been reared upon the soil. We leave it to abolition philosophers to solve the problem, while we assert it as a fact, that but few of the free colored men among us, who have been raised in those States where the laws make all men literally equal, possess the same amount of honesty, virtue and intelligence belonging to those who have always lived among those whom they have been taught to regard as belonging to a superior race. Cox came here from Pennsylvania some fifteen or sixteen years ago, and has acquired a fortune of one hundred fifty thousand dollars. He first went into business with Wilkinson, but soon after opened a shop on his own account. He is a good workman, very attentive to business, and altogether a reliable man. His residence is at the corner of Fifth and Elm streets. He is kind and hospitable at home, and has a host of friends. Mrs. Cox is a fine-looking woman, and was wealthy previous to her marriage.

HENRY ALEXANDER McGEE,[71]

Originally from the Old Dominion, is a dealer in vegetables, and has a stand in Commercial street, between Market and Chestnut. He is worth about twenty-five thousand dollars. He is a good business man, and is much patronized by steamboatmen. Owing to certain reports in regard to the character of his wife before marriage, he is not admitted into the first circles, and consequently lives somewhat retired. To those who have been in the habit of regarding even the most intelligent of the colored race as destitute of proper sensibility in matters pertaining to the domestic virtues, it may appear strange that a bare suspicion of former disregard of the proprieties of life should exclude a family from familiar intercourse with an aristocratic circle; but, in this respect, there is reason to believe that the colored people are more strict than the whites; for it is a notorious fact that among the latter a full purse covers a multitude of sins, and ladies who have forfeited all claims to virtuous respect are admitted as ladies of the *ton.*[72] It was only the other day that one of the white aristocracy flogged his wife for deviating from the path of virtue, and yet the lady is still received into what is called "good society." If she had been tinctured with the blood of Ham, the door would have been closed against her.

LUDWELL LEE.[73]

Here is another of the proscribed. Lee is a dealer in vegetables on Green street, between Main and Commercial. He is good for ten thousand dollars, and worships money with a superstitious veneration. His wife has all the vanity of a peacock, and, like that gorgeous bird, is more ornamental than useful.

JAMES NASH[74]

Is a son-in-law of Johnson, with whom he resides. He is steward of the steamer *J. D. Perry*, a Missouri river packet. He is worth about five thousand dollars. Nash is one of the best and most useful men we have. His manners are easy and polite, and all who know him esteem him for the kindness of his heart and the generosity of his disposition.

MR. AND MRS. TAGGERT.[75]

This worthy couple are new comers from the prolific old State of Virginia, the mother of Presidents and mullatos [*sic*]. They board with Mrs. Lyons, and are received into society without difficulty. The lady is very amiable, and is a pattern of a wife.

GABRIEL HELMS.[76]

Everybody knows Gabriel Helms—Professor Gabriel Helms—an old resident and one of the most intelligent men in the country. If you want to know how he got the title of Professor, I can tell you in a few words: He is an imitative man, and those who have noticed the cut of his whiskers, cannot help admiring the success with which he has imitated the facial ornaments of a certain celebrated saddler on Main street.[77] Well, some years ago, there came to our city a pompous little English dancing master, who hired Concert Hall and stuck up his name as "Professor Wells," teacher of the art and science of hop, skip and jump, particularly the waltz, or the science of genteel hugging.[78] Helms had a shaving shop opposite the Hall, and he put up a sign with the name of "Professor Helms," in gold letters. The joke took, and Helms no doubt made many a dollar by the "take off." Professor Helms lives at his ease at Mrs. Rutgers', and has a fortune of thirty thousand dollars. He has been a very industrious man, and has been twice to California. Age begins to tell on him, as his grizzly locks indicate; but he is yet stout and vigorous, and will doubtless live many years.

FRANK ROBERSON,[79]

Who has a shop under Barnum's Hotel, is one of the talking barbers, and can rattle out more nonsense in ten minutes than any sensible man would believe in a week. In society he is not in the best standing, and he is too great a gossip and meddler to let the affairs of others alone. He is doing a good business, and is worth about five thousand dollars. Frank is another scion of Virginia, but the good old State does not often produce so great a parrot as this knight of the razor.

JAMES THOMAS.[80]

We come now to a man of mark—one who has seen the world, and, like Hamlet, knows a hawk from a handsaw.[81] Thomas is an intimate friend of General Walker, the hero of Nicaragua; and of the many brave men who followed his dilapidated banner into that inhospitable country, none stood higher in his estimation than James Thomas.[82] He is a Tennessean by birth, and is worth some fifteen thousand dollars. He is very genteel in his manners, attentive to business, and is a remarkably fine looking man. At present he is barber on the *Wm. M. Morrison,* and is one of the most popular men on the river. Last summer Thomas worked at Clamorgan's, and it was there that a compliment was paid him by a gentleman occupying the front rank of the statesmen of the West—a compliment well deserved, and of which he may justly feel proud on account of the source. The gentleman remarked to Thomas, that all that prevented him from becoming one of the greatest men of the age was his color. Thomas is a moral man, and his character, moral and intellectual, would do honor to the proudest white man in the land.

ANTOINE CRAKIN,[83]

Who was born and raised here, requires but little to be said in his favor, as he is generally known.

MRS. PELAGIE FOREMAN.[84]

It is with extreme reluctance we speak in terms of disrespect of a lady, but the task we have undertaken demands that we should tell the whole truth, however disagreeable it may be to us, and distasteful to some of our readers. Mrs. Pelagie Foreman was born and raised here, and can command the cool sum of one hundred thousand dollars. I grieve to say that this handsome fortune was accumulated in a manner that may well be called questionable. Like Delilah of old, she sheared the strength of more than one Samson, and now lives upon the fruits of her contraband profession. She is now rather dilapidated, but was in her younger days a fascinating lump of yellow flesh. When a girl, she was very imprudent and quite saucy. The liberal use of her tongue once caused her to be severely cowhided, and the punishment was no doubt beneficial to her in after years. At the outset of her career she was the mistress of a white man, whose character up to that time was without reproach. Enjoying the confidence of his fellow-citizens, he was entrusted with an important public office, and large sums of money passed through his hands. Her extravagance soon embarrassed him, and he found his good name and fortune passing rapidly away. Having every confidence in his yellow Dulcinea,[85] he passed his property over to her, intending to reclaim it after his accounts were adjusted. Here, then, we see the honor of a high-minded man, a high public functionary, a man hitherto untarnished by calumny—all in the power of a frail colored girl. I venture to assert that not one colored woman in five hundred would have been false to the trust reposed in her. Pelagie Foreman, however, saw the man she professed to love—who had treated her with all the tenderness due to a wife—declared a defaulter and a dishonored man; saw his noble nature sink under the disgrace, and refused to give up his own property to save his honor! That man has now gone to his grave, and but few know the history of his private life; a cloud rests upon his name: but upon *hers* hangs a load of infamy dark as the shadow of hell. Pelagie lives on her farm, three or four miles from the city, and frequently comes to town in her carriage. She is an outcast from society, into which all her infamous wealth cannot gain her admittance. She is a great tattler, and seldom speaks the truth when she can invent a falsehood. She has property in the city, and derives a considerable income from her rents.

LONDON BERRY,[86]

Is a steward on the river, and lives on Randolph street, between Twelfth and Thirteenth. He is a good man, his only fault being too great a fondness for cards. He is a man of strong prejudices. He came here from Virginia about thirteen years ago, and has made most of his money by honest industry. His wife is a daughter of Mrs. Pelagie Foreman,[87] and will be worth fifty thousand dollars at her mother's death. She was guilty of a faux pas last winter, which for the present has thrown her out of society. The colored people of the second class gave a ball which she attended, and was consequently not invited to a subsequent ball of the first class. Her husband became indignant at the slight, and tried to create a disturbance, but made nothing by the attempt. They are both no doubt sorry for their conduct, and will be again received next winter and their indiscretion forgiven. She is often seen on Fourth street, in her mother's carriage.

ROBERT SMITH,[88]

Is a large, fine-looking man, proud and dignified in deportment, and nearly dark in color. He keeps a coffee-house on Fourth street, and although he sells intoxicating liquors, no drunkenness is permitted on his premises. When he finds that a man has had as much as he can stand under, he refuses to let him have more. Smith is worth nine thousand dollars. He is a man of good moral habits, and has many friends both among white and colored. He is not received into society on account of his wife.

MARSHALL STARKS.[89]

We now come to one of the chivalry. Colored men are generally peaceably disposed, and are not addicted to fighting. Starks, however, has the hot blood of the cavaliers in his veins, and subscribes to the "code of honor." He has been engaged in two affairs of this kind, in both of which he winged his adversary. The first was nine years ago at Algiers, opposite New Orleans; the other was in California. He keeps a coffee-house on Commercial alley, between Green and Morgan streets, and is worth considerable money. He is the best faro[90] dealer in the country: he went to California and returned with forty thousand dollars, which he won at his favorite game. His wife is a fine-looking woman from Cincinnati. Starks is a good business man, hospitable and kind, but very fond of hoarding money.

MRS. MARGARET BEAUVAIS,[91]

Was until recently one of the leaders of fashion in colored society. Inspired by the demon of envy, she united with Mrs. Nash in spreading slanderous reports derogatory of the fair fame of Miss Theodosia Hazlett, than whom a purer or more innocent girl does not exist. In imitation of the low class of whites, she resorted to the "Joker's Budget,"[92] as a medium for her slanders, but failed in her object, as the young lady stands above suspicion. It is to be hoped that she will learn better manners, and pluck the beam from her own eye, before she attempts to remove the mote from her neighbor's.[93]

THE MISSES REYNOLDS.[94]

These young ladies are from Baltimore. Miss Mary Louise cannot be called beautiful, but is amiable, accomplished and intellectual—rather jealous in her disposition, perhaps, but time will correct this fault. Miss Rebecca is handsome, and plays well on the guitar. She sings like a nightingale, and is one of the brightest ornaments of society.

NORTON REYNOLDS, JR.[95]

Holds an important office in Hickman's shop, and is an excellent workman. He is finely formed, and very neat in his dress. Norton is the brother of the young ladies mentioned above, and is an intelligent, well-informed young man.

JAMES WILLIAMS,[96]

Who is employed at Albert White's, is a thin, yellow man, from Virginia. He is a good workman, but has some habits that cannot be highly commended. He lives fast—drinks fast, and drives fast horses. He is a regular Phaeton [*sic*] in a buggy, and scorns to travel at a slower pace than 2.40 on the Plank road.[97]

THOMAS GUNNELL,[98]

The factotum of Frank Roberson's, is an important individual among the colored bloods—a Count D'Orsey[99] done in bronze. He is consulted on all important occasions; and his advice is indispensable when a yellow belle is to be serenaded, or a dark-eyed brunette to be captivated.

GEORGE CAREY,[100]

Flourishes his razor at Albert White's. He is from Washington City. His father, who is very wealthy, lives in Detroit, and keeps George pretty well supplied with the needful. Carey is a good workman, and has many fine qualities, but is excessively fond of the fair sex. The glance of a bright eye sets his heart in a flutter, and he yields to the witchery of a soft voice as a spirited charger to the pricking of a spur. His ruling passion is fondness for the sex, and the thought of dear woman is never out of his mind, but he seems to be ever poring over the delightful anticipation expressed by the poet:

"As soon as night shall fix her seal
Upon the eyes and lips of men,
Oh, dearest! I will panting steal
To nestle in thine arms again!"[101]

ALLEN GUNNELL,[102]

Is on the steamer *Hesperian,* and is worth about five thousand dollars. He is well formed, has straight hair, and is very popular with all classes. He is genteel in his manners, accommodating in his disposition, and fond of obliging his friends.

HARRIET AND JULIA JOHNSON.[103]

These young ladies are sisters-in-law of Smith, who killed his wife and mother-in-law, and daughters of Edward Johnson. The murderer has wealthy friends, who are trying to obtain his pardon.[104] It is to be hoped that money will not be so potent in its influence as to avert the punishment due to the perpetrator of so revolting a crime as that for which Smith has been sentenced. Harriet Johnson is an accomplished and fascinating young lady, and quite intelligent. Julia, her sister, is pretty, but of variable temperament—at one moment all smiles, at the next all frowns.

JAMES HOLMES[105]

Is steward on the steamer *Morton*. He is worth ten thousand dollars, and is a hard-working man of excellent business qualifications.

JAMES W. THOMPSON,[106]

Is a brother-in-law of Sam. Mordecai, and is steward on the steamer *Moses McClelland*. He is a tall, genteel-looking man, and lives in fine style.

We have thus sketched, in a hasty manner, a few of the prominent traits in the personal history of the Colored Aristocracy of St. Louis. It would have been an easy matter to add facts and incidents sufficient to fill a large volume; and at some future time, when we have more leisure, we may, perhaps, take up the subject again, and enter more into details. We have doubtless omitted many whose names would be an ornament to our pages; and have, in a spirit of charity, purposely overlooked some whose acts are marked by shame and ignominy: but we are compelled to defer until some future time a more full and perfect record of persons whose history is known to us, and whose character, whether good or bad, the public have a right to pass judgment upon.

Our next attempt will be to give a true account of the *second class* of colored people. The number is large, and the developments we shall make will startle many of our white friends. The romantic incidents connected with this subject surpass the wildest dreams of fiction; and the phases of humanity that will be presented will cause some of our philanthropists and philosophers to open their eyes in amazement. For the present we bid the indulgent reader—Adieu.

Annotations

1. "Facile" in this context could mean "fluent" or, more negatively, "superficial." The latter meaning is more likely. Clearly Clamorgan was no fan of Stowe's work.

2. Harriet Beecher Stowe (1811–1896) was the daughter of New England Calvinist theologian Lyman Beecher. Rev. Beecher and his family moved to Cincinnati in 1832 when he became the head of Lane Theological Seminary. In 1836 Harriet Beecher married Calvin Ellis Stowe, a professor at Lane. Lane at this time was a hotbed of antislavery agitation, and Stowe found herself drawn into the debate over abolition. Her growing hatred of slavery was strengthened by a brief visit to a Kentucky plantation where she had the opportunity to observe the "peculiar institution" firsthand. The visit made a deep and painful impression upon her. *Uncle Tom's Cabin, or, Life Among the Lowly* first appeared in serial form in the *National Era* in 1851–1852. It was published as a book in 1852 and was an instant success. It was translated into various languages and adapted for the stage. When proslavery commentators challenged the truth of Stowe's assertions about slavery, she countered with *A Key to Uncle Tom's Cabin* (1853), material on the lives of southern slaves culled from court records, newspapers, and personal correspondence. Elevated to the status of an international celebrity, Stowe made several trips to Europe. In England she was received by Queen Victoria. None of her later novels achieved the success of *Uncle Tom's Cabin.*

3. Stowe's novel, *Dred: A Tale of the Great Dismal Swamp*, was published in 1856. Although it received favorable notices, it did not achieve the enduring popularity of *Uncle Tom's Cabin*. The character of the slave rebel Dred is loosely based on Nat Turner.

4. Solomon Northrup (ca. 1808–1863) was a free man of color from Minerva, New York. He supported his family by farming, working for other farmers in the area, and playing the violin. In 1841 two white men

passing through Minerva persuaded him to join their traveling circus for a few months as a musician. The tour ended in Washington, D.C., when his employers drugged Northrup, beat him, stole his free papers, and sold him into slavery. His new master shipped him off to Louisiana. After several unsuccessful escape attempts, and twelve years in bondage, he enlisted the help of a sympathetic white carpenter. Letters were sent to friends back in Minerva and eventually a member of the family that had owned and then freed Northrup's father intervened. Once back in Minerva, Northrup wrote his story with the help of a white neighbor. *Twelve Years a Slave* was published in 1853 and proved very popular. One of Northrup's kidnappers was arrested but, despite the weight of the evidence against him, was acquitted.

5. Virginia-born Henry "Box" Brown (born ca. 1815) effected one of the most daring and imaginative escapes from slavery. Sent by his master to work in a tobacco factory in Richmond, he lived a life of quasi-freedom for many years, marrying and raising a family. All this ended when his wife and children were sold in 1848. Deeply embittered and determined to escape, Brown found two allies, white shopkeeper Stephen A. Smith and his free black clerk, J. C. A. Smith. The two crated Brown up in a large box and sent him express to the Vigilance Committee in Philadelphia. The odds were weighted heavily against him. Even if he evaded detection, he risked serious injury (at one point the box was stowed upside down) or death from suffocation.

Once safely in the North, Brown embarked on a career as an antislavery speaker. He was joined by J. C. A. Smith, who wisely decided to leave Baltimore. (Stephen A. Smith was jailed when his part in the plot became known). The two enjoyed great success on the lecture circuit, using as their props the famous box and a huge panorama, the "Mirror of Slavery"—paintings on canvas depicting Brown's escape and the horrors of slavery.

With the passage of the Fugitive Slave Law, Brown had good reason to fear for his safety. When he was almost retaken by slave-catchers, he and Smith sailed for England. There Brown published *The Narrative of Henry "Box" Brown, Written by Himself* (1851). In England Brown was in great demand as a lecturer. An able speaker and vocalist, he had a real sense of how to attract an audience. He even had himself crated up and transported by rail from one town to another to publicize his lectures. Eventually he and Smith separated, with charges of double-dealing on both sides. Brown kept the "Mirror of Slavery" but Smith had his own painted and also did well as a lecturer. C. Peter Ripley et al., *Black Abolitionist Papers,* vol. 1, 174–75, 293–301.

6. The verdict of the U.S. Supreme Court in *Dred Scott v. John F. A. Sandford* was handed down on March 6, 1857. Clamorgan probably knew a great deal about the case because it had its origins in St. Louis. He may even have known Dred Scott. The slave Dred Scott had been purchased by army surgeon John Emerson from the family of Peter Blow of St. Louis and taken by Emerson to Fort Armstrong, in the free state of Illinois, and then to Fort Snelling, in what is now Minnesota, part of the old Louisiana Territory north of the Missouri Compromise line of 36°30'. Emerson was eventually transferred back to St. Louis, and there he married Irene Sanford. Emerson died in 1843. His widow received all his property, including Dred, his wife Harriet, and their children, in trust for her infant daughter. Apparently in the mid-1840s Scott tried to buy his family's freedom from Mrs. Emerson, but she refused to sell. It was then that Scott secured the services of a lawyer and received permission to sue for his freedom in the St. Louis Circuit Court.

Scott's counsel argued his residence in a free state and in a territory from which slavery had been banned by the Missouri Compromise made him a free man. The first suit, in which Scott was aided by Henry T. Blow, Peter Blow's son, and Henry's brother-in-law, prominent businessman Joseph Charless, Jr., failed on a technicality. The second trial took place in 1850, by which time Irene Emerson had moved to Massachusetts. The Scotts had been left with her brother, John F. A. Sanford (his name was misspelled 'Sandford' in court papers), and he had entrusted them to his agent, Benammi S. Garland. This time the verdict went in the Scotts' favor, but Garland immediately appealed to the Missouri Supreme Court. The appeal was heard in 1852. Scott and his family were ordered returned to slavery.

Meanwhile, Irene Emerson had married Dr. Calvin Chaffee, an antislavery congressman from Massachusetts. She transferred permanent ownership of the Scotts to her brother, who was now living in New York. At this point antislavery lawyer Roswell Field became involved. Given that Chaffee and Field were abolitionist in their sympathies, there has been speculation that they connived to bring a test case to limit the spread of slavery into the territories. The case was taken to the Supreme Court on the "diversity of citizenship" clause of the federal Constitution. Scott, so Field argued, was a citizen of Missouri and John Sanford a citizen of New York. The case therefore belonged in the U.S. Supreme Court.

In the highly charged political atmosphere in the Supreme Court, an initial move to order the case returned to the state court was abandoned when it became clear two antislavery justices were prepared to award Scott his freedom. The majority ruled against Scott and, in effect, overturned the Missouri Compromise. It was Chief Justice Roger B. Taney who went the furthest, insisting that the Missouri Compromise was unconstitutional, that slavery could not be banned from the territories, that no black person, slave or free, could ever become a citizen, and that "the black man has no rights which the white man is bound to respect." As for Dred Scott, Taylor Blow bought him for a nominal sum and freed him, but he died of consumption a year later. Don E. Fehrenbacher, *Slavery, Law, and Politics: The Dred Scott Case in Historical Perspective,* especially pp. 121–50. Charles Van Ravenswaay, *St. Louis: An Informal History of the City and Its People, 1764–1865,* 406–10.

7. By 1858 the man who had escaped from slavery in Maryland as Frederick Augustus Bailey Washington had become Frederick Douglass (1818–1895), the best-known African American antislavery lecturer on either side of the Atlantic. He had published two autobiographies, *The Narrative of the Life of Frederick Douglass* (1845), and *My Bondage and My Freedom* (1855); undertaken a highly successful lecture tour of the British Isles; spoken in towns and villages throughout the North and the Midwest; and established two newspapers, the *North Star* and *Frederick Douglass' Paper.*

8. The threat of war was with Great Britain. The cause was the failure of the United States to cooperate in suppressing the slave trade. There were howls of protest whenever the Royal Navy tried to intercept and search a suspected slaver flying the Stars and Stripes, even though Congress had made it illegal for American merchants and American vessels to engage in the trans-Atlantic slave trade after January 1, 1808. The issue was very much alive in 1858.

9. France's colonial possessions in the Midwest, north of what is today the state of Louisiana.

10. The English translation of a Native American name for the Mississippi River.

11. A pirogue or piragua was a type of canoe commonly used by the native peoples of the Pacific coast of South America and the Gulf of Mexico. It consisted of two hollowed-out tree trunks bound together. Some of the larger pirogues were used for the coasting trade. The French voyageurs adapted the basic design and constructed vessels for use on the Mississippi. Their pirogues were up to sixty feet in length and were poled along or pulled by men on the riverbanks.

12. According to legend, Romulus, the founder of Rome, decided to find wives for his men from among the neighboring Sabines. The Sabine men

were invited to Rome for a day of games and feasting. After they had been lured away, a raiding party descended upon their settlement and carried off the women.

13. Pocahontas or Matoaka (ca. 1596–1617) was the daughter of Powhatan, the leader of the Algonquin people in the Chesapeake region. She befriended the English colonists in Jamestown and was a frequent visitor to the settlement for some months before the famous episode in which, according to Captain John Smith, she intervened with Powhatan to save him from execution. After Smith's return to England, conflict between the colonists and the Algonquin worsened. Pocahontas was seized as a hostage by the English. While in captivity she converted to Christianity and was given the name Rebecca at her baptism. Powhatan eventually ransomed her, but she refused to return to her own people, preferring instead to marry planter John Rolfe. In 1616 the couple traveled to England, where the "Indian princess" was received at court. The Rolfes were preparing to return to Virginia when Pocahontas died of smallpox. She left a son, Thomas, who became an important figure in Virginia society.

14. The original voyageurs or engagés were men employed by the great French fur-trading companies to travel *(voyager)* into the interior of North America to bargain with the various Indian peoples for pelts. Expert canoemen, who learned the languages of many of the Indian nations and often married Indian women, they played a crucial role not only in trade but also in exploration. By the time Clamorgan was writing, the heyday of the voyageurs was long past and the term was applied fairly loosely to French colonial traders and pioneers.

15. Prompted to write by the passage of the Fugitive Slave Act of 1850, Harriet Beecher Stowe crafted a powerful novel about slavery that engaged northern white readers, few of whom would have considered themselves abolitionists. With its memorable cast of heroes and villains, from the evil planter Simon Legree to the saintly slave Uncle Tom, and its sentimental plot, replete with hairbreadth escapes, deathbed scenes, and reconciliations of long-separated family members, *Uncle Tom's Cabin; or, Life Among the Lowly* proved immensely popular, not only in the United States but also in Europe. In *Uncle Tom's Cabin,* Stowe gave her white readers black characters they could admire and even identify with.

16. Roger Brooke Taney (1777–1864) was born on a tobacco plantation in Calvert County, Maryland. Both of his parents were from wealthy slaveowning families. A second son, he was obliged to carve out a career for himself while his elder brother inherited the family estate. He chose politics and the law. As Andrew Jackson's attorney general he advised the

president to veto the bill to recharter the Bank of the United States, and as his secretary of the treasury he helped him dismantle that institution. In 1835 a grateful Jackson nominated him as an associate justice of the Supreme Court. His position on slavery was equivocal. Like his brother-in-law, Francis Scott Key, he supported African colonization. He even manumitted his own slaves. However, he was convinced of the intellectual inferiority of people of color, and opposed both the tactics and the rhetoric of the radical abolitionists. Taney is best remembered for his opinion in the Dred Scott case. As for Clamorgan's assertion that Taney had "kindred of a darker hue" in Missouri, the standard biographies are silent on that point.

17. The Republican party. Although opposed to the extension of slavery into the territories, few of its supporters advocated immediate emancipation, unless accompanied by colonization outside the United States or legal barriers to keep the races apart.

18. John How (d. 1888), a Democrat originally from Philadelphia, served three terms as mayor of St. Louis in the 1850s. A successful businessman at the time Clamorgan was writing, he ran a tannery and was also the president of several financial institutions. However, unwise speculations after the Civil War led to bankruptcy. During the war How played an important role in bolstering pro-Union sentiment in the city. James Neal Primm, *Lion of the Valley; St. Louis, Missouri,* 157, 177–80, 200, 208, 237, 242, 246, 250.

19. John M. Wimer (1810–1863), a blacksmith of German descent from Virginia, entered politics in St. Louis in the 1840s. A Democrat, he was elected mayor in 1843. He was reelected in 1857 by a coalition appalled at growing Republican pressure for immediate emancipation in Missouri, but by the time *The Colored Aristocracy* was written, he was out of office. When the Civil War began, Wimer was imprisoned for his Confederate sympathies. He escaped, fled to southwest Missouri, and joined the Confederate forces of General Emmet McDonald. He was killed at Hartsville, Missouri, in 1863. Primm, *Lion of the Valley,* 172, 242, 326.

20. When Clamorgan wrote *The Colored Aristocracy,* Kentucky native Benjamin Gratz Brown (1826–1885) had emerged as the leading antislavery politician in Missouri. Brown, a Kentucky native, and Frank P. Blair's cousin (see note 21), moved to St. Louis as a young lawyer in 1849. He soon entered politics and served several terms in the state legislature. In a widely reported speech in 1857 he denounced slavery and called for white Missourians to come out in favor of emancipation. His argument was that slavery retarded economic growth. Hand in hand with abolition should go legislation to promote business, homesteading, and white immigration.

(Brown had a strong following among the German settlers in St. Louis. His assaults on the nativist Know-Nothings had already involved him in a duel.) That same year, when he ran as the Free Soil candidate for governor, he came within five hundred votes of being elected. As editor of the *Missouri Democrat* he transformed that newspaper into a Republican journal.

Brown steadfastly opposed secession, and when war came, he served as a colonel in a volunteer regiment. He was elected to the U.S. Senate in 1863, in place of a secessionist. Brown proved himself increasingly radical. In Missouri he called for immediate rather than gradual abolition. He advocated voting rights for white women and African Americans in the District of Columbia, and the perpetual disfranchisement of Confederates. As for Lincoln's Emancipation Proclamation, he insisted it did not go far enough. After the war, when he returned to Missouri, he modified his stance, especially with regard to the treatment of former Confederates. In 1870 he was elected governor as a Liberal Republican. Two years later, after failing to get the presidential nomination at the Liberal Republican convention, he was forced to settle for the role of Horace Greeley's running mate. By the end of his career Brown had moved into the Democratic camp. William Hyde and Howard L. Conrad, *Encyclopedia of the History of St. Louis,* vol. 1, 250. *Dictionary of American Biography,* vol. 3, 105–7.

21. Attorney Francis Preston Blair, Jr. (1821–1875) came from a prominent Kentucky family and emerged as a force in Missouri politics in the late 1840s. In 1848 he sided with the Free Soil party and eventually became one of its leaders. He was elected to the Missouri state legislature and then, in 1856, to a seat in Congress. It is easy to see why Clamorgan thought so highly of Blair. An opponent of slavery, he manumitted his own slaves. In Congress as a Republican, he resolutely opposed the extension of slavery into the territories. However, he did not do so as a radical abolitionist, but as a gradualist who believed emancipation must be accompanied by the colonization of the former slaves in Central America. Blair had a distinguished military career during the Civil War. Even those who loathed his politics admired his personal courage. During Reconstruction Blair found himself out of step with the Radical Republicans. He left the Republican fold, joined the Democrats, and was presidential candidate Horatio Seymour's running mate in 1868. Primm, *Lion of the Valley,* 187. Richard Edwards and Menra Hopewell, *Edwards' Great West and Her Commercial Metropolis, Embracing a General View of the West and a Complete History of St. Louis,* 563. *Dictionary of American Biography,* vol. 2, 332–34.

22. Henry Taylor Blow (1817–1875) was the son of a planter from Southampton County, Virginia. His father, Peter, moved the family first to Alabama and then to Missouri. Henry graduated from St. Louis University. He became a lawyer but soon gave up the law in favor of business. By the time *The Colored Aristocracy* was published, he was the president of the Collier White Lead and Oil Company, one of the largest enterprises in St. Louis. An old-line Whig, Blow allied himself with the antislavery Free Soil element, eventually joining the Republican party. He was elected to the state senate in 1854 and served four years. In 1860 he was a delegate to the Republican convention in Chicago that nominated Lincoln. He was appointed U.S. minister to Venezuela by Lincoln in 1861 but returned to serve in Congress the following year. He was a delegate to the Baltimore convention in 1864 that renominated Lincoln. In 1869 Grant appointed him U.S. minister to Brazil. Like Frank Blair, he favored emancipation not as a radical abolitionist but as a conservative Whig who believed slavery and the slave economy threatened the well-being of white workingmen. Even so, Clamorgan had good reason to count him as a friend to the black community. Blow and his brother advised Dred Scott, whom they had known for many years, to sue for his freedom. When the Supreme Court eventually ruled against Scott, Blow's brother bought him and manumitted him. Edwards and Hopewell, *Great Metropolis,* 226–27. Hyde and Conrad, *Encyclopedia of the History of St. Louis,* vol. 1, 183. Primm, *Lion of the Valley,* 241. *Dictionary of American Biography,* vol. 2, 391–92.

23. Pelagie Rutgers (ca. 1802–1867) was born Pelagie Baptiste. On April 20, 1820, she married barber St. Eutrope Clamorgan, the author's uncle. Six years later, on February 2, 1826, a widowed Pelagie wed Louis Rutgers. It is not clear exactly when Louis died, although it was sometime between 1845, when he signed a deed disposing of some real estate, and 1851, when Pelagie was first listed in the directory as a widow. Her address from 1854 onward was 319 South Seventh, the well-appointed home (complete with piano) described by Clamorgan.

Pelagie invested her inheritance wisely. In 1860 "Palach Louis Rutgers," as the census-taker wrote her name, was worth sixty thousand dollars. She was described as a sixty-year-old mulatto born in St. Louis. Her household included her twenty-year-old daughter, Antoinette, a white woman of eighty-nine whose place of birth is unknown; a Frenchman who worked as a gardener, and a white friend from Red River, Louisiana, Charles Cahomie. She also had two adopted children, French-born Antoine Emanuel Griveaud and a three-year-old German orphan, Barbara Cungle.

When she made her will a few days before her death, Pelagie provided generously for Cahomie, Cungle, and Griveaud. She left money to her church, St. Vincent de Paul, and to the church's orphanage. She also put money in trust to be given to the city of St. Louis if and when it established an orphanage for African American children. The bulk of her estate passed to Antoinette. Oscar W. Collet, *Index to St. Louis Cathedral and Carondelet Church Marriages,* 14, 90. St. Louis County wills, Book H, p. 248. St. Louis County deeds, Book N3, p. 279; Book O3, p. 187; Book T5, p. 56; Book U5, pp. 4, 580, 597; Book 155, p. 212; Book 158, p. 37; Book 224, p. 26; Book 225, p. 391; Book 236, p. 221; Book 237, p. 26; Book 238, pp. 460, 461, 462; Book 239, pp. 271, 448; Book 246, pp. 258, 259, 260, 526; Book 263, p. 301. U.S. Census, St. Louis (1860), Ward 2, p. 665. St. Louis city census, 1855. St. Louis directories, 1851, 1854, 1857, 1859, 1860, 1864–1867. Loren Schweninger, ed., *From Tennessee Slave to St. Louis Entrepreneur: The Autobiography of James Thomas,* 101–4.

24. Louis Rutgers was the son of Dutch-born Arend Rutgers (1755–1837), who emigrated from Dortrecht with his wife and two of his daughters around 1800. (Another daughter stayed in Holland). He became one of the wealthiest merchants and landowners in St. Louis. Arend's only legitimate son predeceased him, and he was apparently delighted when one of his slaves—he owned several—bore him a son. He named the child Louis, brought him up in his household, freed him, and eventually transferred a substantial amount of real estate to him. He also gave the city of St. Louis land for a graveyard and appointed his son sexton. Louis Rutgers leased some of his land to German truck farmers, and built rental properties. He used the income to buy more real estate throughout St. Louis. The real estate Arend Rutgers had given his son eventually became the subject of a heated legal contest when the merchant's daughters laid claim to it. Proceedings dragged on until after Louis's death. Schweninger, ed., *From Tennessee Slave,* 102–4. Frederic L. Billon, *Annals of St. Louis in Its Early Days under the French and Spanish Dominations,* 481. Van Ravenswaay, *St. Louis: An Informal History,* 115. St. Louis County deeds, Book N2, p. 112; Book O2, pp. 12, 315; Book P2, p. 191. St. Louis County wills, Book C, p. 329.

25. Louis Clamorgan (1820–1851 or 1852) was Cyprian's half brother. Like most of the men in the Clamorgan family, including his uncle, St. Eutrope, the first husband of Pelagie Rutgers, he made his living as a barber and hairdresser. Louis Clamorgan acted as trustee for Pelagie while her second husband was alive because, under Missouri law, a married woman could not hold property in her own right. The specific transaction

Cyprian Clamorgan is referring to may have taken place in 1840, when Louis Clamorgan borrowed substantial sums of money and bought all of Louis Rutgers's real estate in what may have been a fictitious sale designed to protect Rutgers from his creditors. SLGS, *Index of St. Louis Marriages,* vol. 1. St. Louis County deeds, Book N3, p. 279; Book O3, p. 187; Book P2, p. 191. For a detailed account of Louis Clamorgan's life see "The Clamorgans of St. Louis."

26. Antoinette Rutgers (ca. 1842–1897) wanted to marry former slave James Thomas (see note 80), but her mother, herself a former slave, objected strenuously. They eventually married on February 12, 1868, almost a year to the day after the redoubtable Pelagie Rutgers died. Even from beyond the grave Pelagie enjoyed a degree of control over her daughter and the man she knew she would marry. In her will she stipulated that Antoinette's inheritance would be "for her sole, separate, & exclusive use, free from the control, and from all liabilities of any future husband." St. Vincent de Paul, Marriage Register (from 1867), 7. St. Louis County wills, Book H, p. 248.

27. Pelagie Papiche, the daughter of Joseph Papiche and Marie Gross Louis, married Louis Nash, the son of William Nash and Rosalie Glenson, on July 26, 1836. He was twenty-eight and she was eighteen. Louis worked as a boatman or steward. He evidently did well, and he and Pelagie were able to buy a home on Third, between Lombard and Hazel. In 1840 the Nashes had a household of four—Louis, Pelagie, and two children. Louis was dead by 1850, when the census-taker listed Pelagie (he spelled her name "Pelise") as the head of household and the owner of property worth six hundred dollars. With her lived her three surviving children: Maria, age twelve; Louis, ten; and Albert, six. (Another child, Julia Pelagie, born in 1843, had apparently died young). The household also included sixty-nine-year-old Mary Papin, like the Nashes a mulatto native of Missouri. The marriage records of Albert and Louis indicate that Pelagie Nash and her children remained in St. Louis through the upheavals of the Civil War. Both married in the city during the 1860s. Collet, *Marriages,* 61; SLGS, *Index of St. Louis Marriages,* vol. 2. St. Vincent de Paul, Baptismal Register, 1844–1852, 12. St. Louis County deeds, Book W4, p. 193; Book 246, p. 132. U.S. Census, St. Louis (1840), p. 104; (1850), Ward 2, p. 196; (1870), Ward 8, p. 281 (Albert Nash); subdiv. 2, p. 131 (Louis Nash). St. Louis directories, 1840–1841, 1842, 1845, 1857.

28. The widowed Pelagie Nash married riverman Antoine Morin (Clamorgan spelled it "Moran") on February 20, 1857. The details of Morin's parentage are somewhat confused. According to one record, he was the son

of George Morin and Margaret Martigny. Another identifies his parents as Michel Morin and Josephine Aubuchon. (Josephine was the sister of another of Clamorgan's "aristocrats," Antoine Aubuchon.) In 1833, when he was in his teens, Morin allied himself with the wealthy and influential Charleville-Labadie clan by marrying Josephine Labadie. The marriage lasted less than seven years. In the 1840 census Antoine Morin was a widower with one son, Louis. (Two daughters, Louise Catherine and Josephine, had apparently died young). His second marriage ended after little more than a year with his own death. U.S. Census, St. Louis (1840), p. 102; SLGS, *Catholic Baptisms in St. Louis, Missouri, 1765–1840,* 33–34; SLGS, *Index of St. Louis Marriages,* vol. 1; SLGS, *Catholic Marriages in St. Louis, Missouri, 1774–1840,* 29. St. Louis directories, 1845, 1852, 1857.

29. This is a play on line 203, epistle 4 of Alexander Pope's "An Essay on Man," which reads: "Worth makes the man, and the want of it, the fellow."

30. Sarah Hazlett was the widow of Monroe Hazlett. Hazlett came to St. Louis from Virginia, and on August 13, 1838, married Amelie Willi. In 1842 he was listed in the directory as a cook. Over the next few years, with his name mangled in various ways (Haslick, Heslet), he was listed as a riverman and a boatman. In the 1850 census he was working as a cook aboard the steamboat *Sacramento.* The census-taker classified him as black. His age was given as twenty-six, although he was surely older than fourteen when he married for the first time. There is no record of the death of his first wife, his marriage to Sarah, or his own death. He is listed in the directory for the last time in 1851.

Sarah Hazlett appeared in the directory in 1859 as Monroe's widow. She lived at 135 South Third and was a seamstress by trade. In the 1860 census she was described as a mulatto and a native of Missouri. She headed a household that included herself and her two daughters, Theodosia, age eighteen, and Emily, sixteen. The census-taker gave her age as thirty but, in light of Clamorgan's statement and the ages of her daughters, she must have been older, unless Theodosia and Emily were Monroe's daughters by his first wife. Clamorgan implies that Monroe Hazlett never married Sarah. However, had he talked to his own half brother, Henry, he would have learned that she and Monroe had been husband and wife. Since the law in Missouri forbade a married woman to hold property in her own right, it was common practice to appoint a male trustee to hold it for her. Henry Clamorgan was Sarah Hazlett's trustee until the death of Monroe made it possible for her to administer her own estate. A woman who lived with a man but did not marry him faced no such legal restrictions. Collet, *Marriages,* 39. Oscar W. Collet, *Index to Instruments Affecting Real Estate*

Recorded in the Office of Recorder of Deeds, In the County of St. Louis, Mo., vol. 2, 435. St. Louis County deeds, Book T5, p. 14; Book 231, p. 318. U.S. Census, St. Louis (1850), Ward 4, p. 122; (1860), Ward 8, p. 730. St. Louis directories, 1842, 1845, 1847, 1848, 1851, 1852, 1859.

31. This term is ambiguous. It refers to a married woman with an absent husband, and to a woman who has lived with, but never married, one or more men. Clamorgan probably chose to describe Sarah Hazlett as a "grass-widow" to leave intact the "mystery" about her precise status.

32. "Sere" means "dry" or "withered." Clamorgan is quoting *Macbeth,* act 5, scene 3, lines 22–23:

> . . . . My way of life
> Is fall'n into the sere, the yellow leaf.

33. This is Clamorgan's rendering of the first four lines of Byron's "She Walks in Beauty." The original reads:

> She walks in Beauty, like the night
> Of cloudless climes and starry skies
> And all that's best of dark and bright
> Meet in her aspect and her eyes.

34. Clamorgan may have been unaware of the fact that some of the finest private schools for black children, especially girls, in Philadelphia were operated by African American teachers. Several, like the one run by Margaretta Forten, accepted boarders. Students came from all sections of the country, including the South, to attend these academies.

35. Mary Obuchon or Aubuchon was born Marie Beaugenoux, the daughter of Nicolas Beaugenoux, Jr., and Marguerite or Pelagie Quenel. On June 14, 1829, she wed François Aubuchon, the son of Antoine Aubuchon (1750–1798), a white settler from Ste. Geneviève, and Elizabeth or Zabetta Datcherut, a slave whom Aubuchon had purchased and freed. (Elizabeth bore Antoine ten children. Left penniless when he died, she sued his estate, recovering crops she had planted, and various items she claimed were hers by right.)

By 1855 Marie Aubuchon or Mary Obuchon was a widow. The city census taken that year showed her as the head of a household that contained six free people of color, including herself. Five years later, in the federal census, Mary "Obushon" was described as a fifty-one-year-old mulatto nurse. She lived on Columbus, near Marion, in the city's second ward, and owned real estate worth four thousand dollars and personal property valued at five hundred dollars. She shared her home with Alexander Pellerin, age sixty, a mulatto native of St. Louis who worked as a cook on a steamboat, and Pellerin's nieces and nephew, twenty-year-old Elise, and twins Josephine and Sylvester. Marie was listed in the directory for the last time in 1868. St. Louis city census, 1855. U.S. Census (1860), St. Louis, Ward 2, p. 707. St. Louis directories, 1860, 1868; Collet, *Marriages,* 2; Oscar W. Collet, *Index to St. Louis Cathedral and Carondelet Church Burials,* 4. St. Louis County deeds, Book 172, p. 133. Carl J. Ekberg, *Colonial Ste. Geneviève: An Adventure on the Mississippi Frontier,* 226–27. Judith A. Gilbert, "Esther and Her Sisters: Free Women of Color as Property Owners in Colonial St. Louis, 1765–1803," 16, 22.

36. This was a common enough expression and Clamorgan could have picked it up from any one of a number of sources, including Irish playwright John O'Keeffe's *The Irish Mimic; or, Blunders at Brighton* (1795), John Dryden's *Secret Love; or the Maiden Queen* (1667), or Sir Walter Scott's *St. Ronan's Well* (1823) and *Redgauntlet* (1824). It was also reportedly the Prince Regent's description of the ideal wife.

37. By 1860 Margaret Aubuchon, age twenty-five, was the wife of James Bedrevers, a twenty-seven-year-old mulatto who worked as a porter on a steamboat. Like his wife, he had been born in St. Louis. The couple lived next door to Mary Aubuchon. U.S. Census (1860), St. Louis, Ward 2, p. 707.

38. As Clamorgan indicates, Samuel Mordecai settled in St. Louis in the early 1840s. A Kentuckian by birth, he was the son of plasterer Harry Mordecai, one of the wealthiest free men of color in Frankfort, Kentucky. Samuel Mordecai's name appeared in the St. Louis directories many times over the years—as a merchant, a steward, a plasterer, and most often as a barber. At the time *The Colored Aristocracy* was written, the Mordecais were living on Eighth near Hickory, in the city's fourth ward. According to the 1860 census, Samuel, a thirty-eight-year-old mulatto, was the head of a household that included his wife, Mary, three years his junior, from Pennsylvania; and three daughters, Julia, age sixteen, Virginia, seven, and Harriet, five. (An infant, Harry Samuel, had died in New Orleans on January 13, 1850. Another child, Mary Blanche, born in October 1857, had also apparently died young). Three mulatto women also lived with the family. One, Fanny Heckley, was a Kentuckian like Mordecai. The other two, sisters Julia and Martha Robinson, were from Pennsylvania. The census-taker valued Mordecai's estate at almost fifteen thousand dollars.

A decade later daughter Julia had married, but Virginia and Harriet still lived at home. There were now two more children, Mabel, age nine, and Edith, five. (The census-taker recorded Mabel's name as Mary and transformed Edith into Edgar). Benjamin Lee, a black Missourian, age ten, lived with the family.

By 1880 Mordecai had reverted to his father's trade and become a plasterer. He and his family, listed as white, lived on Indiana Avenue. Wife Mary kept house, while daughters Virginia (or Jennie) and Harriet were schoolteachers. Edith was in school, as was a grandchild, Mary McLeod, probably Julia's daughter. Mattie Zieger, a niece of Samuel's from Kentucky, also lived with them, as did Louis P. Clamorgan, Mary's nephew, who had been a member of the household on and off for more than twenty years.

The ties that united the Clamorgans, the Mordecais, and fellow "aristocrat" James W. Thompson (see note 106) are rather complicated. On June 29, 1843, Samuel Mordecai married Mary Eagleson in a ceremony performed in St. Louis by a Catholic priest. The previous year Henry Clamorgan had married Harriet Eagleson, Mary's sister. The Eaglesons were the daughters of fruiterer William Eagleson and Catherine Fillicit. The Mordecais were members of the Church of St. Vincent de Paul. When one of their children was baptized there in the 1850s the priest recorded Mary's last name as "Thompson." To compound the confusion, Cyprian Clamorgan says Samuel Mordecai and James W. Thompson were brothers-in-law. One explanation could, of course, be that Samuel was married twice and that both of his wives had the same first name, but that was not the case. In 1900 the Mordecais told the census-taker they had been married fifty-seven years. Mary reported that she had been born in Pennsylvania, and that both of her parents had been Pennsylvania natives—but Henry Clamorgan's first wife was a Missouri native. Perhaps the Eaglesons had come to St. Louis from Pennsylvania with one infant daughter, and a second, Harriet, had been born in Missouri. But what about James Thompson and his tie to Mary?

Whatever the exact nature of the ties of kinship, the Mordecais concluded a number of business transactions with James Thompson. As for the Clamorgans, they helped Samuel and Mary, and were helped in return in many different ways. In 1846 Henry Clamorgan and another African American barber, James D. Bonner, pledged one thousand dollars to secure a license for Mary to reside in St. Louis (indicating she might have been born in Pennsylvania since, had she been a native of St. Louis, she would not have needed a license). When Henry's first wife and several of his children died, the Mordecais took in young Louis P. Clamorgan. He grew up with their own children and in essence became an adopted son. He never returned to live with his father even when Henry remarried. Samuel and Henry acted as trustee for one another's wives in property deals. They were also business partners for more than a decade after the war.

Samuel Mordecai appeared in the directory for the last time in 1901. Mary is not listed as his widow and may have predeceased him. Mabel and Virginia stayed on at the family home on Texas Avenue for some years. Both were highly regarded teachers in the city's schools: Mabel at the Simmons School and Virginia at the Delaney School. Tiffany Papers, Box 61, folder 6; Box 62, folder 1, MHS. St. Louis Marriage Licenses, vol. 2, 401, and vol. 3, 30. Collet, *Baptisms,* 86; St. Vincent de Paul, Baptismal Register, 1852–1867, 216. St. Louis County deeds, Book X4, p. 94; Book H6, p. 513; Book N6, p. 466; Book U6, p. 200; Book 155, pp. 211, 212; Book 169, pp. 211, 212; Book 170, pp. 537, 538; Book 246, pp. 281, 286, 293. U.S. Census (1850) District 1, Franklin County, Kentucky, p. 39; St. Louis (1860), Ward 4, p. 74; (1870), subdiv. 3, p. 30; (1880), vol. 39, e.d. 207, sheet 21; (1900), e.d. 151, vol. 91, sheet 11. St. Louis directories, 1854, 1857, 1859, 1860, 1864–1866, 1868–1886, 1888–1911. Loren Schweninger, *Black Property Owners in the South, 1790–1915,* 111; Willard B. Gatewood, Jr., *Aristocrats of Color: The Black Elite, 1880–1920,* 16, 117; James de T. Abajian, comp., *Blacks in Selected Newspapers, Censuses and Other Sources: An Index to Names and Subjects,* vol. 2, 670–71. *Missouri Republican,* January 24, 1850, in Lois Stanley, George F. Wilson, and Maryellen Wilson, comps., *More Death Records from Missouri Newspapers, 1810–1857,* 74.

39. Fortuna, the Roman goddess of chance, was generally depicted as blind. She bestowed good or ill luck at random.

40. Thimblerig was a game of chance similar to the three-card trick or the shell game. A thimble-rigger would place a dried pea under one of three thimbles, move the thimbles around, and encourage bystanders to bet on which thimble the pea was under.

41. I have been unable to discover what kind of game of chance the Mexican puzzle was. Presumably it was fairly unsophisticated, since Clamorgan classes it with thimblerig. It may even have been another name for thimblerig. One thing is clear. The authorities in St. Louis considered it disreputable. See *Ordinances of the City of St. Louis, 1861,* 614–17, in Jeffrey S. Adler, "Streetwalkers, Degraded Outcasts, and Good-for-Nothing Huzzies: Women and the Dangerous Class in Antebellum St. Louis," 746.

42. Julia Mordecai.

43. The celebrated French writer Alexandre Dumas (1802–1870), often referred to as "Dumas père" to distinguish him from his son, who was also

a novelist and playwright, was the grandson of a French nobleman and a woman of color from the French West Indies, Marie Dumas. Alexandre's father achieved fame as one of Napoleon's generals, but he died a poor man, and Alexandre was left to shift for himself. Imaginative and highly creative, he embarked on a career as a dramatist. His first play, produced when he was twenty-seven, brought him tremendous acclaim. More plays followed, and then he turned to writing historical novels. Among his best-known works are *The Three Musketeers* and *The Count of Monte-Cristo.*

44. White's first name appears in the records as both "Alfred" and "Albert." Alfred White secured his license to reside in St. Louis in June 1842, three years before the law made it mandatory to have one. He was twenty-four and a barber by trade. He first appeared in the directory (as Albert) in 1847. Three years later the census-taker, who called him Alfred, described him as a thirty-two-year-old mulatto, born in Missouri. White's wife's name was Charlotte; she was twenty-seven and a Missouri native. For the next eight years there is no record of Albert (or Alfred) and Charlotte having lived in St. Louis. This was presumably when they were busy making their fortune in the California goldfields. In 1855 the directory for the gold-rush town of Marysville, California, listed one Albert White as the proprietor of a saloon.

By 1859 Albert White was back in St. Louis, with a barbershop on Targee. As Clamorgan observed, life in the goldfields had been good to the Whites. In 1850 they were worth fifteen hundred dollars. In 1860 they owned real estate to the value of twenty thousand dollars and personal property worth $1,650. This time the census-taker recorded Albert White's place of birth as Ohio, and mistook Charlotte's age by ten years.

The Whites stayed on in St. Louis through the chaos and disruption of the Civil War. In 1870 the directory listed Albert White as a steward; his address was given as 409 Targee. The following year Alfred, a "caterer and restauranteur," was reported to be worth twenty-five thousand dollars. Apparently, the scope of his business activities grew over the years. He suffered losses, but was able to rebound from them. In 1886, in an article on wealthy people of color in St. Louis and elsewhere, the *Cleveland Gazette* reported that "A. G. White, formerly purveyor to the Anchor line of steamers, after financial reverses has . . . retrieved his fortunes and accumulated $30,000." Tiffany Papers, Box 61, folder 6, MHS. U.S. Census, St. Louis (1850), Ward 4, p. 55; (1860), Ward 4, p. 42; (1870), Ward 5, p. 23. Marysville, California, directory, 1855. St. Louis directories, 1847, 1859, 1860, 1870–1879, 1881–1886, 1888–1893. *New York Daily Tribune,* July 6, 1871; *Cleveland Gazette,* October 23, 1886.

45. Charlotte White.

46. Weak or of little importance.

47. Short of money.

48. Barriteer Hickman (his name also appears as Byertere, Baratea, Baratere, and even Barritone, but he spelled it Barriteer when he made his will) was in business as a barber in St. Louis as early as 1845. He arrived in the city just before the passage of the law requiring most free people of color to secure licenses to live in St. Louis. He got his license (as Barritta) on December 22, 1846. It cost him and the two white friends who stood surety for him one thousand dollars. The license described him as twenty-one years of age, and five feet, seven inches tall.

Hickman initially worked from his home at 33 Chestnut. Then, in the early 1850s, he acquired separate business premises at 44 Pine. At the time Clamorgan was writing, Hickman had a barbershop adjoining the city's premier hotel, the Planter's House. He and his family lived at 233 South Third.

In the census of 1850 Hickman's age was given as twenty-three (he was actually a year or two older than this). He was described as a mulatto and a native of Virginia. His worth was estimated at seventy-five hundred dollars. His wife, twenty-one-year-old Mary Jane, was also from Virginia. They had one child, six-month-old Judy. They shared their home with another barber from Virginia, possibly Mary's brother, Alfred J. Anderson, his wife and child, and a nineteen-year-old Irishwoman, Ellen Slattery. Judy Hickman evidently died in infancy. In 1860 she was not listed as a member of the household. However, the Hickmans had two young sons, Barriteer, age seven, and Robert, two. They had also taken into their home another mulatto migrant from Virginia, twelve-year-old Britannia Crump. In 1860 Hickman was worth $5,250.

The Hickmans remained in the city through the Civil War, had four more children (Powhattan Augustus, Mary Claudia, Estella Josephine, and William), and prospered. By 1870 Hickman had amassed real estate worth thirty thousand dollars. He had another one thousand dollars in personal property. Son Barriteer was working as an insurance agent, Robert and Powhattan attended school, and Mary Claudia (transformed into Claude by the census-taker) and Estella were still at home. By the early 1880s the Hickmans could look with pride on their children's achievements. Estella became the second black graduate of the St. Louis high schools. Robert was appointed a deputy sheriff, while Powhattan was a clerk at the post office, then the assessor's office, and eventually the recorder's office. Sadly, though, Barriteer, Jr., died in his late teens or early twenties. Barriteer, Sr., died in 1886. Tiffany Collection, Box 61, folder 16, and Box 63, folder 6. MHS. St. Louis County wills, Book Q, p. 626. St. Louis County deeds, Book 156, p. 500. U.S. Census, St. Louis (1850), Ward 3, p. 352; (1860), Ward 3, p. 84; (1870), 2nd subdiv. p. 133. St. Louis directories, 1840–1841, 1845, 1847, 1851, 1852–1854, 1857–1860, 1864–1878, 1881–1886, 1888–1895. Abajian, comp., *Blacks in Selected Newspapers*, vol. 2, 198.

49. Possibly a reference to Heinrich Boernstein (1805–1892), editor of the German-language daily, *Anzeiger des Westens.*

50. Mary Jane Hickman.

51. Robert Jerome Wilkinson first appeared in the St. Louis directory in 1848 in business, as Clamorgan writes, at 38 Vine. In fact, he had already been living in the city for some years. In 1842 he had an unpleasant taste of the realities of life in a slave state. On February 3 he petitioned the judges of the St. Louis County Court from a jail cell. He explained he had been born a free man in Pennsylvania and had lived there for some years. He had come to Missouri about seven years earlier, in 1834 or 1835. He had recently been arrested for living in the city without a license. Although convicted, he lodged an appeal, but while his appeal was pending he had been arrested again. He insisted he had been "advised & believes himself entitled to remain" in Missouri without a license. He considered his arrest "illegal" and requested a writ of habeas corpus. The judges rejected his argument. He swallowed his pride and bought a license.

Once his legal difficulties were behind him, he set about establishing himself socially and economically in St. Louis. On October 20, 1842, he married Julia Ann Spears. He was twenty-nine, and she was several weeks short of her twenty-eighth birthday. The marriage made Wilkinson a kinsman of Cyprian Clamorgan. Julia was the daughter of George Spears and Theresa Denys or Dennis. Theresa was the granddaughter of one of Jacques Clamorgan's "Negro wives," Esther.

The Wilkinsons prospered. The 1850 census records that Robert was worth eight thousand dollars. His household included his wife, incorrectly identified as a Virginian by the name of Mary; their children, Georgianna, eleven, Mary, seven, and Eliza, three; and three unrelated black barbers from Virginia. (Robert Wilkinson was also described as having been born in Virginia). Assuming the census-taker had recorded Georgianna's age correctly, she was either Robert's child by a previous marriage, or a child born out of wedlock to Robert and Julia. She would have been three years old when the couple married.

In 1852 Wilkinson moved from his barbershop on Vine Street and became a partner of the Clamorgans in their new establishment on Fourth and Pine. The partnership did not last long (perhaps prompting Cyprian Clamorgan's less than flattering comments). Wilkinson soon opened his own shop on Olive Street. In 1860, not content with the simple listing in the directory, he took a half page to advertise the special services he offered. In addition to shaving and "Fashionable Hair Cutting" for adults, he paid "Particular attention . . . to the cutting of children's hair."

The 1860 census indicates a number of changes in the Wilkinson household. Robert's birthplace was now given as Pennsylvania. His wife's name was listed correctly. As for their children, Eliza had apparently died, but Georgianna and Mary or Maria had survived. There was a son, Harry Hotspur, age fifteen in 1860, who had not been part of the household a decade earlier, and there were four children born since 1850—Julia, Eva, Apoline, and Robert. Wilkinson's real estate was valued at six thousand dollars and his personal property at four hundred dollars.

Robert Wilkinson's business survived the Civil War. In 1871 the *New York Daily Tribune* reported he had amassed a fortune of at least twenty-five thousand dollars. However, his family had had its share of tragedy. In 1862 Eva and Apoline succumbed to diphtheria within days of each other. Then their mother died. In October 1863 Robert remarried. His new wife, Caroline Thompson, a widow twenty years his junior with one child, was from Pennsylvania. She bore him six more children.

In time Robert's eldest son, Harry Hotspur, joined the firm of Wilkinson and Co. When Robert died in late 1879 or early 1880, Harry Hotspur took over the business. In material terms the Wilkinsons continued to prosper. However, they could not escape the burden of race. In 1911 Robert's grandson, Albert, was an honor student at the Christian Brothers' College. As *Crisis* editor W. E. B. Du Bois observed, "He is very light and some of the teachers did not know he was colored." However, the Collins-Clamorgan annulment case (see "The Clamorgans of St. Louis") brought the Wilkinsons' family history to the fore. Six white seniors announced they would not take part in the commencement exercises if young Wilkinson were allowed to graduate. The college president responded that they could do as they pleased, but that Wilkinson would get his diploma at the public ceremony. Du Bois commented: "There was no objection to [Wilkinson] whatever until the Clanmorgan [sic] case came up." Tiffany Papers, Box 63, folders 6 and 11; Collet, *Baptisms,* 245; SLGS, *Index of St. Louis Marriages,* vol. 1. "Documents relating to the Esther Claim," Hamilton R. Gamble Papers, MHS. St. Louis County deeds, Book G6, p. 283; Book 155, p. 72; Book 156, p. 30. U.S. Census, St. Louis (1850), Ward 4, p. 54; (1860), Ward 4, p. 47; (1870), Ward 3, p. 250; (1880), e.d. 401, sheet 7 (Caroline Wilkinson) and e.d. 35, sheet 8 (Harry H. Wilkinson). St. Louis city censuses, 1847, 1849. St. Louis directories, 1848, 1854, 1857, 1859, 1860, 1864–1871, 1873–1880, 1882–1886, 1888–1891, 1893–1895. *New York Daily Tribune,* July 6, 1871. *Crisis,* August 1911, 144. *Missouri Republican,* May 12 and May 23, 1862, in Lois Stanley, George F. Wilson, and Maryhelen Wilson, comps., *Death Records from Missouri Newspapers: The Civil War Years (January 1861–December 1865),* 184.

52. Elenius Henley was listed in the 1850 census as "Elinious Henry," a twenty-six-year-old mulatto from Virginia. He lived with his wife, Leonore, twenty-eight, also from Virginia, and their infant son, James. His name appears regularly in the directories. In 1852 and 1853 his barbershop was at 27 Vine. In 1854 he was in partnership with barber Arthur Tappan at the same address. By 1860 he had expanded his interests and was running a combined barbershop and baths at 11 and 13 Vine. He and his family resided at Mrs. Nancy Lyons's boardinghouse on Gratiot. The Henleys now had two more children, Virginia, eight, and Amanda, born February 6, 1860. (Another daughter, Octavia, had died in 1856 at age two months.) According to the census, Henley had $850 in personal property.

Elenius Henley stayed in St. Louis during the Civil War. The 1870 census found him living not with Mrs. Lyons but in a home of his own valued at twelve hundred dollars. Now a widower, he relied on daughter Virginia to keep house for him and for his two younger children, Amanda and seven-year-old Virginius. Elenius's eldest son, James, did well professionally, training as a photographer and printer. Virginius eventually became a cook. As for Elenius, he was still working as a barber in 1881 when he appeared for the last time in the directory. St. Vincent de Paul, Baptismal Register, 1852–1867, p. 338. U.S. Census, St. Louis (1850), Ward 2, p. 268; (1860), Ward 3, p. 182; (1870), Ward 3, p. 236. St. Louis directories, 1852–1854, 1859–1860, 1864–1881. *Missouri Democrat,* September 26, 1856, in Stanley et al., comps., *More Death Records,* 46.

53. There is no mention of a Richard Merrin in the records. However, Clamorgan may have been describing Richard Mancier. In 1850 Mancier, a Virginia native, twenty-one years of age, was living with Albert and Charlotte White. No trade was listed for Mancier, but White and another man in the six-person household were barbers. U.S. Census (1850), Ward 4, p. 54.

54. See note 61.

55. Nancy Lyons was born on March 4, 1815, not in St. Louis, but just across the Mississippi in Illinois. She came to St. Louis with her husband, Charles, in 1844. The following year she traveled to France as a nurse with a

prominent white family. On her return she settled down with Charles, and then, in the early 1850s, the couple went west to the California goldfields. By 1854 Nancy Lyons was back in St. Louis as a widow living in a home on Sixth Street, between Cerre and Gratiot. In 1859, still at the same address, she was operating a boardinghouse. In the 1860 census she was described as a mulatto. Her tenants, all of whom were classed as mulattoes, included barber Elenius Henley and other barbers and steamboatmen.

In her eighties, Nancy Lyons moved to a home on Chippewa Avenue where she was a near neighbor of Henry Clamorgan's widow, Amanda. When Nancy Lyons died in March 1922 she was 107 and the city's oldest resident. A devout Catholic, she attended mass every morning for decades until incapacitated by a fall and failing eyesight. St. Louis Necrology Scrapbooks, MHS. U.S. Census (1850), St. Louis, Ward 4, p. 70; (1860) Ward 3, p. 182. St. Louis directories, 1854, 1857, 1859, 1897, 1910–1911.

56. Charles Lyons, a tall, imposing man of thirty-two, settled in St. Louis in 1844 and found work as a fireman on a steamboat. Lyons was a native of Kentucky, the son of a free man of color and a Seneca woman from upstate New York. He had lived as a free man in Kentucky and Mississippi before moving to St. Louis. Soon after his arrival, Missouri passed a law requiring free people of color to register and secure licenses. The only exemptions were for those born free or manumitted in Missouri, those who could prove they had been residents of Missouri since January 2, 1840, and those who could produce a certificate of citizenship from another state. Lyons did not get a license. He was arrested in November 1846 for failure to comply with the law, convicted, and sentenced to pay a fine of ten dollars, after which he was to be expelled from the state. Lyons appealed, maintaining the new law violated the U.S. Constitution. His appeal was rejected. However, the authorities did rescind the part of the judgment requiring him to leave Missouri, presumably on the understanding that he would get a license. Lyons secured a license on December 22, 1846. He and two friends pledged themselves to pay one thousand dollars. In the 1850 census, Charles and Nancy Lyons were listed as living in the household of Thomas Lewis, a mulatto steward from Virginia, in the city's fourth ward. Charles's age was given as twenty-four, although he was actually thirty-eight. He was dead by 1854. That year's directory listed Nancy as his widow. *Opinion in the Case of Charles Lyons, A Free Negro, Determined in the St. Louis Circuit Court, November Term, 1846*, Antislavery Pamphlets, MHS. Tiffany Papers, Box 61, folder 16, and Box 63, folder 6, MHS. U.S. Census (1850), St. Louis, Ward 4, p. 70. St. Louis directories, 1845, 1847, 1854.

57. Cahokia is in Illinois, across the Mississippi from St. Louis. A settlement was established there in 1699 by French missionaries from Quebec. It took its name from the Cahokia tribe, part of the Illinois Confederacy. The Cahokia had occupied the area for many centuries before the arrival of the Europeans. The French settlement attracted farmers and traders from Canada and Louisiana, some of whom brought slaves with them.

58. The Ottawa chief Pontiac (ca. 1720–1769) was a formidable warrior and an astute statesman. Apprehensive that the removal of the French as a counterweight to the British at the end of the French and Indian War would lead to the wholesale seizure of tribal lands, he devised what the British termed "Pontiac's conspiracy." On a given day in 1763 a confederation of warriors in a vast area from Lake Superior to the lower Mississippi would attack all the British forts. Despite being betrayed, Pontiac successfully laid siege to Detroit. In all, the peoples in his confederation took eight of the twelve forts in the region. The conflict dragged on for three years with neither side victorious, and in 1766 Pontiac made a treaty with the British. In 1769, on a visit to Cahokia, he was murdered by a member of the Peoria tribe.

59. In St. Louis on November 26, 1846, Kentucky native Preston G. Wells married Jane Adams, a migrant from Virginia. Wells made his first appearance in the St. Louis directory in 1851 as the proprietor of the "Nonpareil Hairdressing Saloon and Baths" at 52 North Third. Over the years he was in business as a barber and hairdresser at various locations. In 1850 the census-taker described Wells as a forty-year-old black man. Jane, age thirty-five, was classed as a mulatto. The couple shared their home with two women—a young mulatto from Missouri and a forty-year-old Irish immigrant. A decade later their household included twelve people, since, as Clamorgan indicates, Jane Wells now presided over a boardinghouse. Her age was given as forty-eight, and she was now described as black. Her husband's age was given as sixty. There were two other people by the name of Wells in the household—Barrit, age thirty, a mulatto from Ohio, and Henry, eleven, a mulatto from Missouri. Preston G. Wells held personal property worth three hundred dollars.

As the Civil War drew toward an end, Wells became more vocal than most of Clamorgan's "aristocrats" about the rights of black people in the United States. In 1864 he traveled to Syracuse, New York, to attend the National Convention of Colored Men. He also branched out professionally, becoming a notary public, one of the first black notaries in Missouri. He may have left St. Louis in the late 1860s. Neither he nor his wife appear in the 1870 census, and he was listed for the last time in the 1870 directory. SLGS, *Index of St. Louis Marriages,* vol. 1. *Proceedings of the National Convention of Colored Men, Held in the City of Syracuse, N.Y., October 4, 5, 6, and 7, 1864: With the Bill of Wrongs and Rights, and the Address to the American People,* 6. U.S. Census, St. Louis (1850), Ward 3, p. 379; (1860), Ward 7, p. 152. St. Louis city census, 1849, 1857. St. Louis directories, 1851, 1853, 1854, 1859, 1860, 1864–1866, 1868, 1870.

60. Jane Adams Wells.

61. In Shakespeare's *Othello, The Moor of Venice,* Iago is the ensign to Othello, a Moorish general in the service of the Venetian republic. Othello has married Desdemona, the daughter of a Venetian senator, against her father's wishes. The general passes over Iago, an older and more experienced officer, and promotes his friend, Cassio. Vowing revenge, Iago sets about poisoning Othello's mind, convincing him that Desdemona and Cassio are lovers. In the last act of the play Othello murders Desdemona in a jealous frenzy, only to learn, too late, that she has never betrayed him. Overwhelmed by guilt and despair, he commits suicide. Iago's wife, Emilia, Desdemona's servant, has been an unwitting agent in her husband's plot. When she learns of his villainy she denounces him and he kills her. His crimes discovered, Iago is condemned to a slow death by torture.

62. Identifying the Sawyers with any degree of certainty is not easy. On September 1, 1857, at St. Louis Cathedral, Theresa Helms married one William Sawyer. No one by that name is listed in the city directories for 1857–1860 or in the 1860 census, but in 1859 Francis Sawyer, a pastry cook, lived at 78 Almond, the same address as Gabriel Helms. *He* was married to a woman named Teresa, a Missouri native. In 1860 the Sawyers—Francis, a thirty-two-year-old boat steward from Ohio; Teresa, a twenty-four-year-old chambermaid; Matilda, seven; and Francis, fourteen—boarded with Henry and Emily Spencer, black migrants from Virginia. Given the ages of Matilda and Francis, Jr., they were probably Francis Sawyer's children by an earlier marriage. St. Louis Marriage Licenses, vol. 8, p. 426. U.S. Census (1860), St. Louis, Ward 4, p. 382. St. Louis directories, 1858–1860, 1864, 1866.

63. Born in Missouri in 1808, William Johnson, Sr., was in business for himself as a barber by the time he was in his mid-twenties. He first appeared in the directory in 1836. Thereafter he was listed regularly at various locations throughout the city. By the time *The Colored Aristocracy* was published, he and his family were living at 95 Poplar (later renumbered 311 Poplar) in what Clamorgan suggests was a comfortable home.

On July 29, 1833, Johnson married Mary or Marie Larivière, the sixteen-year-old daughter of Pierre Larivière and Mary Labadie. By 1850 they had six children, five daughters and a son, ranging in age from two to sixteen (another daughter had died young). A decade later there were three more children, the youngest eleven months old, and three grandchildren. Daughter Ellen was now the wife of James Nash (see note 74). The couple and their children lived with her parents, as did daughter Louisa and her husband, James Holmes (see note 105).

As Clamorgan indicates, Johnson had a real flair for making and keeping money. In 1850 he was worth eight thousand dollars. In 1860 his real estate holdings were valued at twenty thousand dollars and his personal property at one thousand dollars. He survived the Civil War with his business interests intact. In 1870 he was in partnership with another black barber, James R. Bosher, on Hammond Street. He remained in business until his death in 1879 or early 1880. Son William, Jr., succeeded him. St. Louis County deeds, Book T2, p. 396. U.S. Census, St. Louis (1850), Ward 2, p. 222; (1860), Ward 4, p. 187; (1870), Ward 5, p. 823; (1880), e.d. 6, sheet 12. St. Louis city census (1849). SLGS, *Catholic Baptisms,* 21, 75. SLGS, *Index of St. Louis Marriages,* vols. 1 and 2. St. Louis directories, 1836–1837, 1838–1839, 1840–1841, 1845, 1847, 1848, 1851–1860, 1870–1877, 1879–1884.

64. William Johnson, Jr., is not listed in the censuses of 1850 or 1860. As for the St. Louis directories, only one contains a reference to a man of color by the name of William Johnson who might have been the elder Johnson's nephew, although it could just as easily be a reference to Johnson, Sr. In 1840 one William Johnson was in business with Louis Clamorgan in a "family grocery" at the corner of Third and Poplar. St. Louis directory, 1840–1841.

65. Antoine Joseph St. Pierre Labadie and his brother, Pierre, repeatedly left census-takers and compilers of directories confused as to their racial identity. The fact that they were wealthy and were very obviously members of the prominent Labbadie or Labadie clan, kin to the Chouteaus and the Gratiots, the white aristocracy of St. Louis, compounded the problem.

As Clamorgan notes, Antoine prospered as a butcher and cattle dealer. His name first appeared in the city directory in 1841. For many years he was in business on Second Street, but by the mid-1850s he and his family had moved to a home on Clark Avenue.

On January 6, 1829, when he was in his early twenties, Antoine married nineteen-year-old Julie, the only child of Jonathan Baptiste Irbour dit Mathurin and Susanne Jeanette, a free woman of color. Mathurin and

Susanne Jeanette lived together for many years but did not marry until he was on his deathbed. Mathurin divided his estate between his "dear and much loved legal wife" and their daughter. Seventeen years later, when her mother died, Julie inherited the entire estate.

Antoine and Julie had nine children, several of whom died young. In the 1850 census (in which the family was listed as white) Antoine headed a household that consisted of himself, Julie, and three of their children, Julie, eight, Peter, six, and Louis, two, as well as Rosalie Jacquet, a twenty-four-year-old Missouri native whom Julie eventually adopted. Antoine Labadie, a "gentleman," owned real estate and personal property worth fifteen thousand dollars.

A decade later Labadie, now described as a mulatto cattle dealer, was worth more than forty thousand dollars. The household was essentially the same, except that the Labadies' eldest son, twenty-eight-year-old Antoine, also a cattle dealer, had returned from California to live with the family. (He eventually settled in New Mexico.)

Antoine, Sr., died in 1862, leaving his entire estate, including property in Illinois, to Julie. She survived him by many years. In 1870 her household consisted of herself, her daughter, Julie, and Rosalie Jacquet. Her real estate was valued at fifty thousand dollars. All three women were described as mulattoes.

Julie Labadie died in 1888, having outlived all but one of her children by Antoine. Under the terms of her will, son Peter received one dollar, and the heirs of son Antoine got one dollar apiece. The home on Clark and Fifteenth in which Julie had lived for so many years went to Rosalie, along with all its contents. What looked like evidence of a family quarrel was nothing of the sort. Julie still owned a substantial amount of real estate inherited from her mother, and under the terms of Susan Jeanette's will that would be passed on to the Labadie heirs. Julie was providing in the only way she could for Rosalie, who, as an adopted child, could not share in the Mathurin-Jeanette estate.

The complex history of Antoine, Julie, and their children is made more complex by the fact that Labadies and Labbadies, some white and some mulatto, were scattered throughout the city. In 1860, for example, Mary Labadie, a thirty-six-year-old woman of color with real estate worth twenty-five hundred dollars, kept house for Gabriel Chouteau, one of the richest white businessmen in the city. Before he married Pelagie Nash, Antoine Morin (see note 28) was married to Josephine Labbadie. They had a son, Louis, and when Louis was left an orphan he moved in with the family of Louis Charleville (see note 67). Charleville, a wealthy butcher and Pierre Labadie's sometime business partner, was married to Louisa Labbadie. Determining how the members of the Labadie clan were related to each other is no easy matter, given the preference of white and mulatto family members for using just a handful of first names. St. Louis County wills, Book A, p. 341; Book C, p. 194; Book G, p. 147; Book T, p. 34. St. Louis County deeds, Book O3, p. 403; Book 239, p. 271. U.S. Census (1850), St. Louis, Ward 2, p. 213; (1860), Ward 4, pp. 46, 133; (1870), Ward 5, p. 26. SLGS, *Catholic Baptisms,* 23. Collet, *Marriages,* 42, 45; Collet, *Burials,* 58. St. Louis directories, 1840–1842, 1845, 1847, 1851, 1854, 1859–1860, 1864, 1867, 1869, 1871, 1873–1874, 1876–1879, 1881, 1883–1888. William E. Foley and C. David Rice, *The First Chouteaus: River Barons of Early St. Louis,* 211–12. Gilbert, "Esther and Her Sisters," 15, 20, 23. Abajian, comp., *Blacks in Selected Newspapers,* vol. 2, 437; Abajian, comp., *Supplement,* vol. 2, 1.

66. Peter Labadie (born ca. 1810) began business as a butcher in partnership with Louis Charleville in 1842, but soon branched out on his own. That he prospered is evident from the fact that in 1846 he was able to pledge one thousand dollars to help a friend, John Washington, secure his license to live in St. Louis. In 1849, listed as a free man of color, Labadie headed a household that included three white men and two free women of color. The following year he shared a home in St. Louis's third ward with several other mulatto butchers. He left St. Louis some time after 1852, and in 1860, listed as a white man, he was a resident of St. Clair County, Illinois. He was married to forty-year-old Felicité, from Tennessee, and they had adopted a young orphan from Missouri, John High. Labadie employed three white servants. His farm was valued at six thousand dollars, and he owned an additional nine hundred dollars' worth of personal property. U.S. Census (1850), St. Louis, Ward 3, p. 319; (1860), St. Clair County, Illinois, p. 327. St. Louis city census, 1849. St. Louis directories, 1842, 1845, 1851, 1852. Tiffany Papers, Box 61, folder 16, MHS.

67. Louis Charleville (b. 1805) was the son of Louis and Adelaide Charleville. On November 26, 1827, he married Louise Julie Labadie, daughter of Joseph Labadie dit St. Pierre and Geneviève Labuche. The Charlevilles had three children—Louisa Adelaide (born 1830), Louis (born 1832), and Joseph (born 1834).

Louis Charleville commenced business as a butcher in 1836. He entered into partnerships with several white merchants. In 1859 he was in business as a butcher with Stephen Sanborn, and in 1860 with Conrad Mast as a provision merchant. Charleville, Sanborn, and Mast collaborated in a number of real estate deals.

Charleville was a wealthy man (apart from a crisis in the mid-1850s when he borrowed money from Henry Clamorgan and lost a substantial portion of his real estate when he could not repay the loan). He was also a generous man. He had no need of a license to live in St. Louis because he had been born in Missouri. However, he helped several other men of color get their licenses by standing surety for them.

In the 1830 census the Charlevilles were listed as white. Over the years officials would be confused again and again as to their racial identity. In 1860 the census-taker classified fifty-five-year-old Louis as a mulatto. His estate was valued at thirty thousand dollars. With him lived his wife, Louisa; sons Louis, a confectioner, and Joseph, a butcher; a mulatto laborer; and three white immigrants. His next-door neighbor was kinsman Antoine Labadie, the brother of another former business partner, Pierre Labadie.

At some point during or immediately after the war Charleville bought a farm outside the city. In 1870, worth nineteen thousand dollars, he was living as a farmer in Central Township. His household members were his wife, their three children, all of whom were unmarried, and five young Missouri natives, ranging in age from four to nineteen, by the last name of Cozen. Charleville employed a blacksmith, a female domestic from Ireland, and a farm laborer from Holland. Every member of the household was classed as white.

Charleville's sons carried on the family business when he died. In 1886 a correspondent to the *Cleveland Gazette* described the Charlesville [sic] brothers as prosperous "butchers and stock drovers." Collet, *Marriages,* 17, 45; Collet, *Baptisms,* 44. Tiffany Papers, Box 61, folders 13 and 14, MHS. St. Louis County deeds, Book Z3, p. 288; Book 153, p. 462; Book 155, pp. 213, 465; Book 170, pp. 537, 538; Book 173, p. 7; Book 225, pp. 86, 112, 414; Book 236, p. 403; Book 237, p. 401; Book 238, p. 193; Book 239, p. 107; Book 263, p. 546. U.S. Census, St. Louis (1830), p. 359; (1860), Ward 4, p. 46; (1870), Central Township, Mo., p. 190. St. Louis directories, 1836–1837, 1842, 1848, 1851–1852, 1854, 1857, 1859–1860, 1866, 1879–1882, 1885–1886, 1888–1896, 1898–1899. *Cleveland Gazette,* October 23, 1886.

68. Irish-born Peter Richard Kenrick (1806–1896) became Bishop of St. Louis in 1843, and Archbishop in 1847.

69. In Shakespeare's *The Merry Wives of Windsor,* Abraham Slender, Justice Shallow's cousin, attempts to woo wealthy Ann Page at Shallow's suggestion. So inept is Slender that Shallow and Welsh parson Sir Hugh Evans have to conduct the courtship for him. Ann Page elopes with another

man. Louis Charleville met with a similar lack of success. Antoinette Rutgers did not marry either of his two sons.

70. Barber Peter Cox was in business with fellow Pennsylvanian Robert J. Wilkinson (see note 51) at 39 Vine from 1845. By 1851 he had opened his own establishment on Green Street. He subsequently moved to 106 North Third. The family home was on Myrtle. St. Louis directories, 1845, 1847, 1851, 1854, 1857, 1859–1860.

71. Henry Alexander McGee secured a license to live in St. Louis in December 1846. He was twenty-eight years old and a "boat furnisher." As a supplier of provisions for steamboats, he prospered as the city's river trade grew. In 1848 he had a vegetable store on Commercial Street. By 1854 he had moved to 177 Eighth, and by 1857 he owned a home and business premises at 121 North Eighth. In 1857 his household included himself, his wife, and two other free people of color. McGee remained in St. Louis during the Civil War. Within months of the Union victory he chaired a meeting of free men of color that issued an address to "the friends of equal rights" asking for civil and political equality. He was listed in the directory for the last time in 1865. St. Louis city census, 1857. St. Louis directories, 1848, 1854, 1857, 1859, 1865. Tiffany Papers, Box 63, folder 6, MHS. *An Address of the Colored People of Missouri to the Friends of Equal Rights, October 12, 1865,* in Philip S. Foner and George E. Walker, eds., *Proceedings of the Black State Conventions, 1840–1865,* vol. 2, 279–82. Lawrence O. Christensen, "Black St. Louis: A Study in Race Relations, 1865–1916," 321.

72. Fashionable society (French). Clamorgan may be indulging in a play on words. The "ladies of the *ton*" he describes are not far removed from "women of the town" or common prostitutes.

73. The census-takers and compilers of directories were often defeated by Ludwell Lee's name. He appears variously as "Ludley," "Tredwell" and "Leedwell." As "Ludwell," the thirty-three-year-old Virginia native secured a license to live in St. Louis on February 8, 1847. It cost him and his friends $250. The license described Lee as five feet, four and one-half inches tall, and a porter by trade.

Lee may have been a humble porter in 1847, but he quickly carved out a niche for himself in the produce trade. By 1850 he was worth three thousand dollars. According to the city census of 1857, the river provided him with a handsome living. The steamboats that plied the Mississippi needed to be provisioned, and Lee established himself as a "furnisher of steamboats." Owners, masters, and stewards of vessels would call at his produce cellar at 14 Green to place their orders. The trade proved lucrative. By 1857 Lee was the owner of the store on Green Street and a two-story brick house at 373 Eleventh. In 1860 his estate was worth twenty-six hundred dollars.

Lee married twice. When the federal census of 1850 was taken, his wife was a thirty-seven-year-old Virginian, Emilie. The couple had two children, Margaret, age ten, and William Henry, seven. A decade later Emilie was dead and Lee was married to another Virginian, thirty-eight-year-old Mary, the woman Clamorgan described as having "all the vanity of a peacock."

The Lees remained in St. Louis through the Civil War. By 1870, worth almost thirteen thousand dollars, Ludwell had retired from business. Mary gave her occupation as "seamstress" and informed the census-taker she had personal property of her own worth one hundred dollars. Apparently the Lees did not fare well in the late 1870s and early 1880s. Their fortunes probably declined as the trade on the river diminished. By 1881, when he appeared in the directory for the last time, Ludwell Lee had resumed his old occupation. He was working as a porter. The following year his son, William Henry, was listed as a porter.

Interestingly, in the 1850 census everyone in the family was described as black. In 1860 Ludwell and Mary were mulattoes, but Ludwell's children were black. In 1870 Ludwell was black and Mary mulatto. As for Lee's connections back in Virginia, there was a white dentist named Ludwell G. Lee, age thirty-five, living in Lynchburg in 1850. Tiffany Papers, Box 63, folder 6; Box 62, folder 2, MHS. U.S. Census, St. Louis (1850), Ward 4, p. 31; (1860), Ward 10, p. 439; (1870), Ward 11, p. 461; Lynchburg, Va. (1850), p. 88. St. Louis city censuses, 1847, 1849, 1857; St. Louis directories, 1848–1849, 1851, 1854, 1857, 1859, 1860, 1864–1867, 1870–1872, 1880–1882.

74. James Nash appeared in the 1854 directory as a steamboatman; he lived at 233 South Third in "the yard." By 1859, when he had moved in with his Johnson in-laws, he was a steward. A year later the directory listed him as a provision dealer. In the 1860 census he was described as a huckster. He owned real estate worth $350 (although he was still living with his wife's family) and personal property worth $500. He and his wife, Ellen, had three children—Laura, age four, Kate, three, and Nancy, three months. Ten years later the Nashes were living next door to the Johnsons. James was working as a barber. The census-taker was hopelessly confused when it came to noting down the names of the various members of the household. Mrs. Nash's first name was recorded as "Mary," but she matched Ellen Johnson Nash in age and place of birth. The Nashes' eldest child, Laura,

was listed, as were four young sons, Alfred, Daniel, Joseph, and Paul. Nancy was renamed "Barella." As for the Nashes' remaining daughter (or daughters), Kate, who appeared in the 1860 census, had been replaced a decade later by "Alice," supposedly born in 1859. There is a discrepancy in terms of ages. Alice is a year or two younger than Kate, and it is, of course, possible that Kate had died young, but that does not explain why Alice, who was alive when the 1860 census was taken, did not appear in it. What happened to Ellen Nash and her children at the hands of the census-taker serves as an object lesson in the perils of believing everything in the census! St. Louis directory, 1851, 1854, 1859–1860, 1864, 1871, 1878–1879. U.S. Census, St. Louis (1860), Ward 4, p. 187; (1870), Ward 5, p. 823. Schweninger, *Black Property Owners,* 123.

75. The 1859 city directory listed William Taggert as a steward. As Clamorgan noted, Taggert and his wife boarded with Nancy Lyons on Sixth, near Gratiot. Eventually, though, they acquired a home of their own at 1404 Gay Street. William Taggert worked for several years for William Roberson, barber Frank Roberson's brother (see note 79) and himself the proprietor of a barbershop. Taggert left Roberson's employ in 1872 and worked at a restaurant. For some years he was a porter, and then he returned to the river as a steward. His name appeared in the directory for the last time in 1884. St. Louis directory, 1859, 1864, 1869–1880, 1882, 1884.

76. South Carolinian Gabriel Helms (1801–1879) was connected by marriage with other members of the "aristocracy." On December 29, 1831, Gabriel "Alloms" (his name defeated the French-speaking clerk at St. Louis Cathedral) married fifteen-year-old Matilda Selina Spears. Matilda was a great-granddaughter of Esther, Jacques Clamorgan's onetime mistress. The marriage made Helms a family member (in a roundabout way) of the Clamorgans. When Robert J. Wilkinson married Matilda's elder sister, Julia, it made Helms and Wilkinson brothers-in-law.

Gabriel Helms first appeared in the St Louis directory of 1838–1839 as a barber, with an establishment at 105 South Third. In 1845 he was in partnership at 20 Chestnut with one Richard Helms, who boarded with him. Clamorgan's statement that Helms had twice gone to California is borne out by his absence from the directories between 1848–1850 and 1852–1858. Presumably he made one trip during the height of the Gold Rush and another a few years later. The evidence for a first trip with at least part of his family in 1849 or 1850 is supported by census data. In 1850 one "Gabriel Helm," a sixteen-year-old black youth from South Carolina, was working as a cook for three white men in Sacramento. He was probably the barber's son. Another son, Samuel, born in Missouri in 1833, was working as a barber in El Dorado, California, in the early 1850s.

Matilda Helms died young, after what may well have been a stormy marriage. Gabriel fathered two illegitimate children: Augustina, who took his last name, and George Hamilton. He did not remarry after Matilda's death. In 1858, perhaps newly returned from the West Coast, he boarded with Mrs. Rutgers, but by 1860 he had moved out and made a home for himself and his children, twenty-year-old Augustina, and three of his children by Matilda: Joseph, age eighteen, Emma, fourteen, and Louis, twelve. Helms was described as black and his children as mulatto. His real estate was valued at ten thousand dollars, and his personal property at a modest forty dollars. A decade later he was living alone. Retired from business, he had an estate valued by the census-taker at fifteen thousand dollars.

By virtue of his age, his decades-long residence in the city, and his intimate knowledge of the doings of the members of his community, Gabriel Helms was the ideal witness in a case the Clamorgans brought in 1875 to try to recover land they claimed had belonged to Jacques Clamorgan. Helms died four years later, leaving a will that suggests a certain estrangement from his children: he considered them "all . . . of improvident habits." He left legacies to three of his legitimate children, Joseph, Gabriel, and Theresa (now Mrs. Sawyer); and to his two illegitimate offspring, Augustina and George Hamilton. There is no mention of his other children, Emma, Louis, or Samuel. They had either predeceased their father or had been disinherited by him for one reason or another. St. Vincent de Paul, Marriage Register (from 1867), 6. Collet, *Baptisms,* 244, 245. SLGS, *Catholic Baptisms,* 19. SLGS, *Catholic Marriages,* 1. St. Louis County wills, Book N, p. 58. St. Louis County deeds, Book T, p. 349; Book X2, p. 441; Book I2, p. 410; Book P3, p. 212; Book Z3, p. 397; Book 157, p. 363. U.S. Census (1850), Sacramento, Calif., p. 165; (1860), St. Louis, Ward 4, p. 201; (1870), Ward 3, p. 195, and Ward 8, p. 186. St. Louis directories, 1836–1837, 1838–1839, 1845, 1847, 1851, 1859–1860, 1865–1866, 1870–1872, 1875–1879, 1881, 1884–1886, 1889–1895. Abajian, comp., *Blacks in Selected Newspapers,* vol. 2, 185. Christensen, "Black St. Louis," 321.

77. The saddler was Thornton Grimsley, inventor of the dragoon saddle, a well-known figure in the social life of the city, and politician Henry Taylor Blow's father-in-law (see note 22). St. Louis directory, 1859. Van Ravenswaay, *St. Louis, An Informal History,* 220.

78. The unfortunate target of Gabriel Helms's wit was one W. G. Wells, who advertised himself as a "professor of music and dancing" in the

St. Louis directory for 1838–1839. Van Ravenswaay, *St. Louis, An Informal History,* 348.

79. Clamorgan gave this individual's name as "Roberson." However, it often appeared as Robinson or Robison in directories and official documents. Francis Robinson, a barber, twenty-four years old, and five feet, five inches tall, secured his license to reside in St. Louis in August 1848. He was first listed in the directory as a barber in 1851. In 1854 he entered into a partnership with Brooklyn, Illinois, resident James M. Boyd. The two operated a barbershop and baths at 106 North Third. That partnership had been dissolved by 1857 when Roberson was listed as working on his own in a barbershop in the basement of Barnum's Hotel. In 1860 the firm of "F. Robinson and Bro." was formed when Francis took his brother, William, into business. In time another brother, Robert, joined them. On December 15, 1857, Francis Robison (as his name was listed on the marriage certificate) married Illinois native Susan V. Turner.

The Roberson brothers remained in St. Louis during the war. At war's end Frank added his voice to those of other prominent men of color in an appeal to "the friends of equal rights" for full citizenship and an equal role in government. He did well professionally, adding chiropody to barbering. William also prospered, amassing ten thousand dollars from his "baths, shaving-saloon, and accompanying branches of business." Robert, if somewhat less wealthy, also operated a successful barbershop. Tiffany Papers, Box 63, folder 6, MHS. SLGS, *Index of St. Louis Marriages,* vol. 1. U.S. Census (1850), St. Louis, Ward 3, p. 399; (1870), Ward 5, p. 5 (William and Robert Roberson), p. 17 (Frank Roberson). St. Louis directories, 1851, 1852, 1854, 1857, 1859, 1860, 1876–1878, 1881–1884, 1888–1889, 1892–1895. *An Address of the Colored People . . . to the Friends of Equal Rights,* in Foner and Walker, eds., *Proceedings of the Black State Conventions,* vol. 2, 279–82. Christensen, "Black St. Louis," 321. *New York Daily Tribune,* July 6, 1871.

80. James Thomas was born in Nashville, Tennessee, in 1827, the son of a slave, Sally Thomas, and a prominent white jurist, John Catron. Catron, who ended his career as a U.S. Supreme Court justice, did nothing for his son. It was left to Sally Thomas to free him. Working as a laundress, she scraped together \$350 of the \$400 demanded for his freedom. A sympathetic planter, Ephraim Foster, lent her the rest. She repaid him, but, in order to circumvent the law that required freed slaves to leave the state or forfeit their freedom, James became legally Foster's property.

As a child, James helped Sally in her laundry and attended a school for free people of color in Nashville. He also gained valuable work experience.

From a white physician he learned dentistry and bloodletting, and from a slave barber he learned the art of dressing hair and trimming beards. At age nineteen he opened his own barbershop. He did well and his clientele included some of the most distinguished citizens of Nashville.

Thomas made two trips to the North as the personal attendant to a wealthy planter. On the first trip he was still legally a slave, and he was continually being urged by northerners to seize his chance and escape. However, he had friends and family and a business back home. Moreover, after several encounters with the virulent racism of the "free" North, he had no wish to stay.

Eventually, Thomas approached Ephraim Foster and secured his legal freedom. Then, relying on his reputation as a hard-working and reliable member of the community, and the friendship of many in Nashville's white elite, he successfully petitioned to be exempted from the law that required him to leave the state.

Despite his material success, Thomas was restless. In 1855 he visited New Orleans. On his return he was intrigued by news of the exploits of filibuster William Walker in Nicaragua. He and his nephew set off to join Walker (see note 82). Once back in Nashville, Thomas did not stay put for long. His travels took him to Wisconsin, back to Tennessee, to Iowa, and then to Kansas. In 1857 he arrived in St. Louis. There he found work as a steward on a steamboat and as a barber in Henry Clamorgan's shop. He eventually became Clamorgan's partner.

Soon after his arrival, Thomas met Antoinette Rutgers. He converted to Catholicism and joined the church of St. Vincent de Paul, where she and her mother worshiped. Handsome, wealthy, and with excellent prospects, Thomas was a good match for Antoinette, but her mother disapproved. Like Thomas, Pelagie Rutgers had been born a slave, but she refused to allow her daughter to wed a former bondsman. Only after Pelagie's death could the two marry.

With his own savings and his wife's money, Thomas embarked on a career as a real estate broker. He acquired a large number of valuable properties and proved, as he had done in the past, that he was a shrewd and resourceful man of business. By 1870 he was the richest person of color in Missouri. One report put his wealth at half a million dollars. The Thomas home on Seventh Street was elegant and well-appointed. It contained, among other things, the piano from the Rutgers home about which Cyprian Clamorgan had so much to say. The Thomas household also included many of the dependents Pelagie Rutgers had supported.

In 1873, at the height of his prosperity, Thomas traveled to Europe as a gentleman of leisure. He was pleasantly surprised to discover few Europeans shared the racial attitudes of white Americans. Once back in St. Louis, he dissolved his partnership with Clamorgan and opened an elegant barbershop and baths at the new Lindell Hotel. His place of business was described by one reporter as "The handsomest barbershop in the world." Profits from the barbershop and various rental properties were invested in yet more real estate. The Thomases gave generously to a wide range of religious, charitable, and educational institutions intended to benefit both black and white citizens of St. Louis. They also patronized African American artists. One of their acquisitions was a statue of the Virgin by sculptor Edmonia Lewis.

In 1877 the Thomases bought a new home across the Mississippi in Alton, Illinois, and it was there, in modest comfort, that they raised their family. They had five children: James Lewes Rutgers, Pelagie Sarah Theodosia (who died in infancy), Eliza or Pelagie, John, and Joseph. By the late 1880s James Thomas began to make plans to retire. However, he lost heavily in the Panic of 1893. His fortunes were starting to recover when a tornado struck St. Louis, severely damaging much of his rental property. Then Antoinette fell ill and died. The family estate was encumbered and the house in Alton, along with its contents, was auctioned off. Thomas went to Chicago to live with daughter Eliza, who had married and moved there. Eventually, he salvaged some of his property in St. Louis, moved back to the city, and settled in a small apartment at 616 Rutger Street. He had begun making notes for his autobiography in Alton. Now he worked on putting his jottings together into a coherent memoir. The task occupied him until his death in 1913. By the time of his death the Rutgers-Thomas estate had dwindled to almost nothing. His personal effects were valued at a meager $1.45. Schweninger, ed., *From Tennessee Slave,* 1–19. Abaijian, comp., *Supplement,* vol. 2, 462. St. Vincent de Paul, Marriage Register (from 1867), 7; Baptismal Register, 1852–1867, 74, 155, 352. St. Louis County deeds, Book 492, p. 323. U.S. Census (1870), St. Louis, Ward 3, p. 195; (1880), Madison County, Illinois, vol. 39, e.d. 10, sheet 15. *New York Daily Tribune,* July 6, 1871; *Cleveland Gazette,* October 23, 1886. St. Louis directories, 1864, 1866, 1868, 1875–1877, 1879, 1881–1889, 1893–1911.

81. *Hamlet,* act 2, scene 2, lines 369–70: "I am but mad north-north-west. When the wind is southerly I know a hawk from a handsaw."

82. In 1853, with a motley band of followers, Nashville native William Walker landed in Mexico, declared Lower California and Sonora an independent republic, and appointed himself head of state. Driven out by the

Mexicans, he returned to the United States and in 1855 invaded Nicaragua. He became the nation's president in 1856. However, opposition from a coalition of Central American states proved too strong, and Walker was forced to surrender and return home in 1857. Before year's end he was back in Nicaragua, but that expedition ended in failure. His last attempt at filibustering occurred in Honduras in 1860 and ended in his death.

James Thomas apparently knew the "Filibuster" and his family in Nashville. When Thomas and his nephew, John H. Rapier, Jr., sailed to Nicaragua in 1856, Thomas carried with him a letter to Walker from his father. Thomas was lured to Nicaragua, as were many others, by the promise of free passage, land, and money. Reflecting on his experiences when he was an old man, he wrote: "When I was going to Nicaragua people would ask, what are you going there for? I thought it strange to put that question to me when such grand opportunities were presented . . . But before I left [Nicaragua] I was asking myself what did I come here for? The thing of it being uncertain about getting anything to eat, either morning, noon or night, with the prospect of the thing getting worse, was no rosy path. I did learn that there is a great deal in Immajination [sic]." Walker was perfectly willing to welcome the two African American freebooters, but Thomas's enthusiasm waned when he learned Walker planned to reintroduce slavery to the area he controlled. Thomas and Rapier returned home, but Thomas remained in contact with Walker. The Filibuster's brother tried to persuade Thomas to go back to Nicaragua, and Walker himself urged Thomas to join him on a second foray. Schweninger, ed., *From Tennessee Slave*, 8–9, 131–42, 204, 207. *Dictionary of American Biography*, vol. 20, 363–65.

83. Antoine Crevier (Clamorgan misspelled his last name) was a prominent member of the "colored aristocracy." Born in 1809, he was the son of Antoine François Crevier (1752–1829) and Catherine Belai. The older Crevier was a longtime resident of St. Louis, and appeared in the first directory, published in 1821. On August 30, 1836, when he was twenty-seven, the younger Crevier married sixteen-year-old Hélène Tayon, the daughter of Jonathan Tayon. In 1854–1855 the directory listed Crevier as a steward on a steamboat; the family home was on the corner of Spruce and Eighth. By 1860 Crevier had abandoned the river, at least temporarily, and was working at the Clarendon Hotel as a hairdresser.

In 1850 Crevier, described by the census-taker as a thirty-five-year-old mulatto (he was in fact forty-one), headed a household that included himself; his wife, "Ellen," a mulatto; and six-year-old Sylvester Crevier, categorized as black. In 1860 the census-taker listed Crevier (whom he called "Cravy") as a thirty-year-old mulatto barber. His wife's age was given as thirty-nine. Both were classed as mulattoes. They shared their home with Mary Mennard, a fifty-one-year-old mulatto from Missouri. Crevier owned real estate worth four thousand dollars and $150 in personal property. According to the 1870 census, Crevier, now listed as black, was a retired laborer. The value of his real estate had declined to $1,150 and his personal property was worth $350. His household included himself, his wife (also described as black), and a six-year-old mulatto, Sylvester Cravier [sic]. It is not clear whether the Sylvester of the 1870 census was the son of the Sylvester listed two decades earlier. Quite possibly the older individual was Antoine Crevier's son and the younger his grandson. Antoine was listed in the directory for the last time in 1874, and Hélène for the last time in 1882. U.S. Census, (1840), St. Louis, p. 149; (1850), Ward 2, p. 258; (1860), Ward 4, p. 343; (1870), Ward 4, p. 525. Collet, *Marriages,* 19; Collet, *Burials,* 25. St. Louis directories, 1821, 1854–1855, 1860, 1864–1866, 1871–1872, 1874–1879, 1881–1882.

84. The woman Cyprian Clamorgan knew as Pelagie Foreman went by several names. She was born Pelagie Lacroix in Missouri around 1810. She eventually anglicized "Pelagie" as "Eliza," and took the name "Foreman" in the late 1820s or early 1830s when she was living with the man who fathered her eldest daughter, Virginia Foreman (born in 1830 or 1831). On September 24, 1849, as Eliza Lacroix, she married Augustus Holland, a man of color fourteen years her junior from Maryland. Holland worked as a foreman in a chemical factory in St. Louis. The couple had two children, Augustina (who was born in 1849 or 1850), and Josephine (who was born in 1853 or 1854 and died young).

As Clamorgan indicates, Eliza Holland was a shrewd businesswoman. She took the money that came her way over the years and invested it in real estate. She owned a farm in Central Township, a few miles outside St. Louis, and property in the city, much of which she settled on her daughters, Augustina and Virginia (now Mrs. Berry). Augustus Holland died in June 1863. Eliza never remarried. In 1870 Mary (as Eliza now called herself) and Augustina were living on her farm with the Berrys, their two children, and three servants. By the time the next census was taken, Augustina had married, borne two children, and been widowed. Mary or Eliza Holland apparently sold her farm and she, Augustina, Augustina's children, and the Berrys moved to the city. U.S. Census (1860), Central Township, St. Louis County, p. 798, and St. Louis, Ward 3, p. 189; (1870), Central Township, p. 181; (1880), St. Louis, vol. 42, e.d. 437, sheet 14. St. Louis directories, 1854–1855, 1859, 1860. St. Louis County deeds, Book U3, p. 186; Book

D4, p. 303; Book 230, p. 63. *Missouri Republican,* June 3, 1863, in Stanley et al., comps., *Missouri Death Records: The Civil War Years,* 82.

85. Beloved. In Miguel de Cervantes' *Don Quixote* the knight calls his lady, the peasant Aldonza Lorenzo, "Dulcinea del Toboso" (Dulcinea of the washtub).

86. On November 7, 1845, Virginia native London Berry and his surety, white ship chandler William C. Anderson, Jr., paid a two-hundred-dollar bond to secure Berry the right to live in St. Louis. Berry, age twenty-five, five feet, seven and one-half inches in height, and of a "rather light Complexion," was described as a "Stewart [sic] on a Steam boat." He was literate. On September 17, 1846, Berry, "a free Mulatto," married Virginia Foreman, "a free Mulatto Girl," in a Catholic ceremony.

Berry first appeared in the directory in 1848. He and his wife lived on Austin Street, and then on Poplar. By the time *The Colored Aristocracy* was written, they had a home on Randolph, between Thirteenth and Fourteenth. Berry had paid five thousand dollars for the property in 1856. Thanks to the generosity of Virginia Berry's mother, Eliza Lacroix or Eliza Holland (the woman Clamorgan knew as Pelagie Foreman), they also owned several adjoining lots.

The Berrys do not appear in the 1850 census, but they have the unusual distinction of being listed twice in 1860. London, Virginia, and their thirteen-year-old son, William, were included in Eliza Holland's household in Central Township, and in their own household in Ward 3 in St. Louis. Virginia's stepfather, Augustus Holland, boarded with them in the city.

In 1870 the Berrys were living with Virginia's mother and sister in Central Township. In 1880 London and Virginia and their sixteen-year-old daughter, also named Virginia, were living on Sublette Avenue, in a home that included London's mother-in-law, his widowed sister-in-law, Augustina Alexander, her two daughters, and two male boarders. Berry was still listed as a steward on the river. He died in 1882 or early 1883. Tiffany Papers, Box 63, folder 7, MHS. St. Louis County deeds, Book 170, p. 328; Book 172, p. 526; Book 230, p. 63. U.S. Census (1860), Central Township, St. Louis County, p. 798, and St. Louis, Ward 3, p. 189; (1870), Central Township, p. 181; (1880), St. Louis, vol. 42, e.d. 437, sheet 14. St. Louis directories, 1845, 1848, 1851, 1854, 1857, 1859–1860, 1864–1866, 1874–1875, 1880–1883. St. Louis Marriage Licenses, vol. 3, 319.

87. Virginia C. Foreman was baptized on August 9, 1835, when she was about seven years old. She was the daughter of Eliza Lacroix, a free woman of color (see note 84) and a Mr. Foreman, presumably one of Eliza's

wealthy white lovers. Virginia was eighteen when she married twenty-six-year-old London Berry. She was listed in the St. Louis city directory as Berry's widow in 1883, indicating her husband had died in 1882 or in the early months of 1883. She outlived him by at least fifteen years. Collet, *Baptisms,* 93. St. Louis directories, 1883, 1886–1899.

88. In 1850 the census-taker listed Robert Smith as a thirty-five-year-old black boatman from Virginia. He presided over a household that included himself; his brother, Alexander, age thirty; and his wife, Hester, a forty-year-old mulatto from Virginia. In reality, Hester was Smith's mistress. Her name was Hester Sisco. The two did not marry until November 4, 1852.

In 1854 the Smiths lived at York House, at the corner of Second and Greene. By 1857 they were running a boardinghouse on South Fourth. There is every indication that they were doing well, for they owned the two-story brick building they lived in. Possibly the fact Robert Smith now owned real estate (worth twelve hundred dollars) and had a successful business carried weight with the census-taker in 1860. He categorized Smith, who had been black a decade earlier, as a mulatto. Apparently the Smiths employed and catered to fellow Virginians. In 1860 everyone in the household, staff and boarders alike, was from Virginia with the exception of a steamboat steward from Washington, D.C. (There is some discrepancy regarding the ages of the Smiths. In 1850 Robert was thirty-five, Hester forty, and Alexander thirty. A decade later Robert was forty-two, Hester thirty-eight, and Alexander twenty-seven.) SLGS, *Index of St. Louis Marriages,* vol. 1. U.S. Census, St. Louis (1850), Ward 3, p. 360; (1860), Ward 4, p. 194. St. Louis city census, 1855, 1857. St. Louis directories, 1854, 1857, 1859, 1860.

89. According to the St. Louis city census, in 1855 Starks headed a household that included himself and two other free people of color, a man and a woman. The federal census-taker in 1860 recorded Starks's name as Marshall Starks Corcoran. He was described as a thirty-three-year-old mulatto from Missouri. His wife, Rebecca, age twenty-three, was, as Clamorgan indicated, originally from Ohio. They had four children: Lavinia, four, Marshall, three, Rebecca, one, and two-month-old Walter. Starks's or Corcoran's real estate was valued at twenty-four hundred dollars and his personal property at eight hundred dollars. He employed a female servant. The coffee-house, described in the directory as a billiard saloon, was on Commercial Street, but the Starks family had a separate dwelling on Clark Avenue, between Fifteenth and Sixteenth. They were neighbors of the Charlevilles and Antoine Labadie.

The Starks family stayed in St. Louis through the upheavals of the war. In 1870 Marshall was still running a saloon, although the value of his real estate had fallen to one thousand dollars. He and Rebecca were now the parents of seven children, including young Frémont, named for the Union commander who championed abolition. By 1874 Starks had given up his saloon and his occupational status had declined markedly. The directory listed him as a porter. In 1881, when he appeared in the directory for the last time, he was a cook. U.S. Census, St. Louis (1860), Ward 4, p. 47; (1870), Ward 5, p. 29. St. Louis city census, 1855. St. Louis directories, 1859, 1860, 1867–1870, 1874–1875, 1877, 1881.

90. A card game in which players bet on the order in which certain cards will appear when taken one at a time from the top of a pack. On the dishonest nature of faro and the dubious moral reputation of those who played it, especially the dealers, see Ann Fabian, *Card Sharps, Dream Books, and Bucket Shops: Gambling in Nineteenth-Century America,* 21–22.

91. There is no reference in any of the records to a woman of color named Margaret Beauvais. There was a family of jewelers and silversmiths in St. Louis by the name of Beauvais in the 1850s, but evidently all of its members were white.

92. The *Joker's Budget and Mysteries of St. Louis,* edited by Rufus M. Underwood, was a scurrilous weekly that printed gossip by and about the inhabitants of St. Louis. The second half of the publication's title may have been Underwood's attempt to capitalize on a successful and highly controversial novel of the same name. *The Mysteries of St. Louis* by Henry (or Heinrich) Boernstein (see note 49) was a virulent attack on the Jesuits. Underwood began publication of the *Joker's Budget* in 1852. As Clamorgan implies, it was hardly a respectable journal. Its gossip columns and its cartoons were calculated to offend, and it carried advertisements for brothels and gambling dens. It annoyed and outraged so many citizens that it was officially suppressed in 1868. Robert C. Boyd, "Literary Activity in Antebellum St. Louis," 68, 107–8; Hyde and Conrad, *Encyclopedia of St. Louis,* vol. 3; Van Ravenswaay, *St. Louis, An Informal History,* 448–49.

93. Matthew 7:2: "And why beholdest thou the mote that is in thy brother's eye, but considerest not the beam that is in thine own eye?"

94. Rebecca and Mary Louise Reynolds were the daughters of Norton and Mary Reynolds of Baltimore. The 1850 census for Baltimore's sixth ward lists Norton Reynolds, Sr., as a mulatto seaman, age thirty-nine. He and his wife were both natives of Maryland. They had five children: Rebecca, age sixteen, William, fourteen, Norton, thirteen, Mary Louise, eleven, and Billy, eight. In 1858, when Clamorgan wrote *The Colored*

Aristocracy, Rebecca would have been twenty-four and Mary Louise nineteen. U.S. Census (1850), Baltimore, Ward 6, p. 208.

95. In 1860 Norton E. Reynolds was living in the household of Charles Prichard, a thirty-three-year-old black barber from Pennsylvania. Norton's age was given as twenty-one, although he was actually twenty-three. Reynolds remained in St. Louis through the war, married, and prospered. His first wife, Mary, was from Illinois. By 1870 Norton and Mary were the parents of three children, William, Joseph, and Mary. Norton was in business as a barber and had a modest estate valued at eighteen hundred dollars. He and all the members of his household were described as white. By 1880 Mary was dead and Norton had married again. (The Reynolds family appears twice in the 1880 census). Like his first wife, his second, Virginia, was from Illinois. They had a young daughter, Maude or Blanche, born in 1878. Another daughter, Letitia, was born in 1882.

Over the years, Norton Reynolds and his children did fairly well financially. Reynolds worked for Henry Clamorgan, and then went into business for himself. When Henry Clamorgan died, Reynolds joined forces with Clamorgan's partner, Joseph Roeser, and took over the Clamorgan barbershop and baths at 407 Pine. He continued to operate it when Roeser retired or died. Son Joseph followed in his father's footsteps and became a barber, while daughter Mary taught school. U.S. Census (1850), Baltimore, Ward 6, p. 208; (1860), St. Louis, Ward 7, p. 38; (1870), Ward 3, p. 241; (1880), vol. 38, e.d. 99, sheet 4; vol. 42, e.d. 39, sheet 14; (1900), vol. 90, e.d. 144, sheet 8. St. Louis directories, 1859, 1864–1865, 1870–1872, 1874–1875, 1877–1879, 1881–1886, 1888–1899.

96. James Williams is hardly an uncommon name, and that complicates the task of identifying the man Clamorgan is referring to. In December 1846 James Williams, a forty-year-old drayman, secured a license to reside in St. Louis. He was probably the same individual who, according to the city census of 1849, presided over a household composed of himself, his wife, and their two children. It may have been another James Williams, also a man of color, who was listed in the 1854 directory as a barber. His address was Washington Avenue, between Thirteenth and Fourteenth. Five years later he was living on Fourth and Pine. Tiffany Papers, Box 63, folder 6, MHS. St. Louis city census, 1849. St. Louis directories, 1854, 1859.

97. In Greek mythology Phaethon was the half-mortal child of the god Helios, whose task it was each day to drive a fiery chariot through the skies to warm and illuminate the earth. Helios rashly allowed Phaethon to drive the chariot for a day. Lacking his father's immortal strength, he lost control of the horses. Veering from its accustomed course, the chariot

came too close to the earth, threatening it with destruction. The king of the gods, Zeus, intervened, killing Phaethon with a thunderbolt.

Plank roads were introduced to the United States from Canada in the 1840s. They were built by laying planks across wooden supports. Deep ditches were dug on either side to prevent the roads from flooding. An 1859 map of St. Louis indicates that there was a plank road on the northern outskirts of the city, in the tenth ward. Presumably this is the one on which James Williams liked to drive. Caroline E. MacGill et al., *History of Transportation in the United States before 1860,* 299–305.

98. No one of this name appears in any of the available records.

99. Alfred Guillaume Gabriel, Comte D'Orsay (1798–1852) was an arbiter of fashion in London and Paris for many years. Born in Paris, the son of one of Napoleon's generals, he served in the French army. A chance meeting with the Earl of Blessington led to an invitation to join the English nobleman and his family on a tour of Italy. D'Orsay eventually married fifteen-year-old Harriet Gardiner, Blessington's daughter by his first marriage, but on the death of the earl he abandoned Harriet for the widowed countess. Their London home became a literary and artistic center. D'Orsay enjoyed a reputation as a great wit and a gifted painter and sculptor. A fervent supporter of Louis Napoleon during the French king's exile in London, D'Orsay eventually joined him in Paris when he was restored to the throne. The move was prompted as much by loyalty as it was by the count's bankruptcy. The king's favor waned, but it was sufficient, along with D'Orsay's acknowledged skill as an artist, to secure him the position of Director of Arts in Paris.

100. George Carey is listed in the 1850 census as a twenty-three-year-old black "Boy" aboard the steamboat *El Paso.* His place of birth is given as Kentucky. He ran afoul of St. Louis authorities in 1855 when he was arrested and fined for living in St. Louis without a license. He could have been expelled from the city, but he was not. By 1860 he was working for Henry Clamorgan in his barbershop and baths at 50 1/2 North Fourth. He was still employed by Clamorgan in 1868, the last time his name appears in the directory. Tiffany Papers, Box 63, folder 13, MHS. U.S. Census (1850), St. Louis, Ward 4, p. 151. St. Louis directories, 1860, 1864, 1868.

101. Extensive research has failed to identify the author of these lines. They may have been written by Clamorgan himself, perhaps in imitation of Lord Byron, whose poetry he much admired.

102. Missouri native Allen Gunnell secured his license to live in St. Louis in May 1862, when he was thirty-four. The document described him as a "bright mulatto," five feet, four inches tall, with a "slender form." He was

literate. In fact, although he did not get his license until 1862, Gunnell had been living in St. Louis since 1857, when the directory listed him as living at 11 Vine, the same address as fellow barber Elenius Henley. Three years later he was employed at the fashionable King's Hotel. He made his home in St. Louis and met his wife, Ellen Harris, there. The couple were married on July 1, 1867. The Gunnells enjoyed a degree of stability unknown by many citizens of St. Louis irrespective of race in the years after the Civil War. They lived in the same home at 3037 Lambdin for a quarter of a century. Allen Gunnell was still working as a barber in 1899. U.S. Census, St. Louis (1860), Ward 6, p. 279. St. Louis directories, 1857, 1859, 1865, 1870–1872, 1874, 1878–1882, 1884–1899. SLGS, *Index of St. Louis Marriages,* vol. 2. Tiffany Papers, Box 63, folder 5, MHS.

103. The Johnson sisters do not appear in any of the available records. Their father may have been one of the two men of color by the name of Edward Johnson listed in the 1859 directory. Edward Johnson was a drayman in business on Austin, near Fourteenth. Edward T. Johnson was a hairdresser on Green, between Second and Third. St. Louis directory, 1859.

104. I could find no mention of a double murder having been committed in St. Louis in the 1850s by anyone named Smith (assuming the crime took place in St. Louis).

105. In November 1852, with the help of white commission merchant Unit Rasin, James Holmes raised five hundred dollars to pay for his license to live in St. Louis. He was twenty-two and apparently illiterate; he could not sign his name on the bond. However, as Clamorgan indicates, he did well over the next few years. By 1860 he had married Louisa Johnson, daughter of affluent barber William Johnson, Sr. (see note 63). When the *Morton* was in port, Holmes lived with his in-laws on Poplar Street. The Holmes family remained in the city through the war, and James left the river. After a stint as a porter, he was in partnership as a barber with another man in the firm of Randolph and Holmes. James Holmes died relatively young. In the 1874 directory Louisa was listed as a widow. She and her four children, Charles, Selina, John William, and Agnes, continued to make their home with her parents. U.S. Census, St. Louis (1860), Ward 4, p. 187; (1870), Ward 5, p. 823; (1880), e.d. 6, sheet 12. Tiffany Papers, Box 62, folder 5, MHS. St. Louis directories, 1851, 1860, 1871–1872, 1874, 1879.

106. In 1853 steward James W. Thompson married Catherine M. Vashon. The Vashons were a prominent African American family in western Pennsylvania. Catherine was the daughter of John Bathan Vashon,

a veteran of the War of 1812, and the sister of lawyer and educator George Boyer Vashon (1824–1878). This was a family committed to education. John B. Vashon sent one of his daughters, perhaps Catherine, to Philadelphia to attend noted African American teacher Sarah M. Douglass's private school. In the 1880s Catherine's widowed sister-in-law, Susan Paul Vashon, and her children settled in St. Louis. Three nephews and a niece secured appointments as teachers in the public schools, and the family established itself firmly in the "colored aristocracy."

Clamorgan notes that James Thompson and Samuel Mordecai were brothers-in-law, but the exact details of the relationship are difficult to work out. Mordecai was married to Mary, whose last name was sometimes given as Eagleson and sometimes as Thompson! She is described as having been born in Pennsylvania in some records and as a Missouri native in others. She was also apparently the sister of Henry Clamorgan's first wife, Harriet. However, Cyprian does not indicate that Thompson and Henry Clamorgan were brothers-in-law. Whatever the nature of the familial ties, James W. Thompson was close to the Mordecais, as evidenced by a number of property transactions with them over the years. St. Louis Marriage Licenses, vol. 6, p. 318. U.S. Census, St. Louis (1860), Ward 4, p. 74. St. Louis directories, 1859, 1885–1886, 1890–1891. SLGS, *Index of St. Louis Marriages,* vol. 1. St. Louis County deeds, Book N6, p. 466; Book U6, p. 200; Book 155, p. 212; Book 170, p. 538. Gatewood, *Aristocrats of Color,* 117–18. William Cooper Nell, *The Colored Patriots of the American Revolution,* 182–87. Catherine M. Hanchett, "George Boyer Vashon, 1824–1878: Black Educator, Poet, Fighter for Equal Rights," 205–19, 333–49.

Bibliography

Manuscript Collections

Alexian Brothers Archives, Elk Grove Village, Ilinois
- Patient Registers of the Alexian Brothers' Hospital, St. Louis, 1900–1907

Church of St. Vincent de Paul, St. Louis, Missouri
- Parish Registers, 1844–1932

Missouri Historical Society
- Jacques Clamorgan Papers
- Hamilton R. Gamble Papers
- St. Louis City Census, 1847, 1849, 1855, 1857
- St. Louis Necrology Scrapbooks
- Walter B. Stevens Scrapbooks
- Tiffany Papers

National Archives, Washington, D.C.
- Third Population Census of the United States (1810)
- Fourth Population Census of the United States (1820)
- Fifth Population Census of the United States (1830)
- Sixth Population Census of the United States (1840)
- Seventh Population Census of the United States (1850)
- Eighth Population Census of the United States (1860)
- Ninth Population Census of the United States (1870)
- Tenth Population Census of the United States (1880)
- Twelfth Population Census of the United States (1900)
- Thirteenth Population Census of the United States (1910)

St. Louis, Archives of the City and County
- Deeds
- Marriage Licenses
- Probate Records

Newspapers and Periodicals

Cleveland Gazette
Cleveland Plain Dealer
Crisis, The
New York Daily Tribune
St. Louis Republic

Law Cases

United States Supreme Court

Isaac Landes, Plaintiff in Error, v. Joshua B. Brant. 51 U.S. Reports 348 (1850).
John Glenn and Charles M. Thurston, Appellants, v. The United States. 54 U.S. Reports 250 (1851).
United States v. Clamorgan. 101 U.S. Reports, 822 (1879).

Missouri Supreme Court

Charles Collins v. Pauline Clamorgan. 5 MO 273 (1838).
Collins v. Adm'r of Clamorgan. 6 MO 170 (1839).
Clamorgan et al. v. Lane. 9 MO 447 (1845).
Clamorgan v. O'Fallon and Lindell. 10 MO 77 (1846).
Landes et al. v. Perkins. 12 MO 151 (1848).
Henry Clamorgan et al., Defendants in Error, v. Isaac T. Greene, Plaintiff in Error. 32 MO 285 (1862).
Clamorgan, Appellant, v. The Baden and St. Louis Railway Company. 72 MO 139 (1880).
Clamorgan et al., Plaintiffs in Error, v. Hornsby et al. 94 MO 83 (1887).
Clamorgan et al., Plaintiffs in Error, v. D. C. Hornsby et al., Defendants in Error. 13 MO Appeals (1883).

Congressional Hearings

House Committee on Private Land Claims. *Claim of Heirs of Jacques Clamorgan. House Bill 17888, 61st Congress.*

City Directories

Marysville, California, 1855
St. Louis, 1821–1914

Additional Printed Sources

Abajian, James de T., comp. *Blacks in Selected Newspapers, Censuses and Other Sources: An Index to Names and Subjects.* 3 vols. Boston: G. K. Hall, 1977.

———. *Supplement.* 2 vols. Boston: G. K. Hall, 1985.

Collet, Oscar W. *Index to Instruments Affecting Real Estate Recorded in the Office of Recorder of Deeds, in the County of St. Louis, Mo.: Grantors.* 3 vols. n.d.

———. *Index to Instruments Affecting Real Estate Recorded in the Office of Recorder of Deeds, in the County of St. Louis, Mo.: Grantees.* 2 vols. n.d.

———. *Index to St. Louis Cathedral and Carondelet Church Baptisms.* 1918.

———. *Index to St. Louis Cathedral and Carondelet Church Burials.* 1918.

———. *Index to St. Louis Cathedral and Carondelet Church Marriages.* 1918.

Congressional Record. 61st Cong., 2d and 3d sess.

Featherstonehaugh, George W. *Excursions through the Slave States, from Washington on the Potomac, to the Frontier of Mexico; With Sketches of Popular Manners and Geological Notices.* New York: Harper and Brothers, 1844.

Documents, Legislative and Executive, of the Congress of the United States, in Relation to the Public Lands, from the First Session of the First Congress to the First Session of the Twenty-Third Congress. Washington, D.C.: Duff Green, 1834. Rpt., Easley, S.C.: Southern Historical Press, 1986.

Foner, Philip S., and Ronald L. Lewis, eds. *The Black Worker: A Documentary History from Colonial Times to the Present.* Philadelphia: Temple University Press, 1978.

Foner, Philip S., and George E. Walker, eds. *Proceedings of the Black State Conventions, 1840–1865.* Vol. 2. Philadelphia: Temple University Press, 1980.

Guinther, Virginia L. "Deaths Reported in the *St. Louis Globe-Democrat,* 1883." *St. Louis Genealogical Quarterly* 27 (winter 1994): 119–21.

Nasatir, A. P., ed. *Before Lewis and Clark: Documents Illustrating the History of Missouri, 1785–1804.* St. Louis: St. Louis Historical Documents Foundation, 1952. 2 vols.

Nell, William Cooper. *The Colored Patriots of the American Revolution.* Boston: Robert F. Wallcut, 1855. Rpt., New York: Arno Press, 1968.

Opinion in the Case of Charles Lyons, a Free Negro, Determined in the St. Louis Circuit Court, November Term, 1846. N.p., 1846.

Prince, R. H., and C. F. DeLauriere. *Petition of Clamorgan's Representatives.* Washington, D.C., 1818.

Proceedings of the National Convention of Colored Men, Held in the City of Syracuse, New York, October 4, 5, 6, and 7, 1864: With the Bill of Wrongs and Rights, and the Address to the American People. Boston: J. S. Rock and George L. Ruffin, 1864.

Ripley, C. Peter, et al., eds. *The Black Abolitionist Papers.* Vol. 1. Chapel Hill: University of North Carolina Press, 1985.

St. Louis Genealogical Society. *Catholic Baptisms in St. Louis, Missouri, 1765–1840.* St. Louis, 1982.

———. *Catholic Marriages in St. Louis, Missouri, 1774–1840.* St. Louis, 1982.

———. *Index of St. Louis Marriages.* Vol. 1 (1764–1854) and vol. 2 (1860–1876). St. Louis, n.d.

———. *St. Louis and St. Louis County, Missouri Probate Records.* 4 vols. St. Louis, 1989.

Schweninger, Loren, ed. *From Tennessee Slave to St. Louis Entrepreneur: The Autobiography of James Thomas.* Columbia: University of Missouri Press, 1984.

Stanley, Lois, George F. Wilson, and Maryellen Wilson, comps. *Death Records from Missouri Newspapers: The Civil War Years (January 1861–December 1865).* Greenville, S.C.: Southern Historical Press, 1990.

———. *More Death Records from Missouri Newspapers, 1810–1857.* Greenville, S.C.: Southern Historical Press, 1990.

Title Papers of the Clamorgan Grant, of 536,904 Arpens of Alluvial Lands in Missouri and Arkansas. New York: T. Snowden, 1837.

[Willson, Joseph]. *Sketches of the Higher Classes of Colored Society in Philadelphia by "A Southerner."* Philadelphia: Merrihew and Thompson, 1841.

Secondary Works

Adler, Jeffrey S. "Streetwalkers, Degraded Outcasts, and Good-for-Nothing Huzzies: Women and the Dangerous Class in Antebellum St. Louis." *Journal of Social History* 25 (summer 1992): 737–55.

———. *Yankee Merchants and the Making of the Urban West: The Rise and Fall of Antebellum St. Louis.* New York: Cambridge University Press, 1991.

Bellamy, Donnie D. "Free Blacks in Antebellum Missouri, 1820–1860." *Missouri Historical Review* 67 (January 1973): 198–226.

———. "The Persistency of Colonization in Missouri." *Missouri Historical Review* 72 (October 1977): 1–24.

Berlin, Ira. *Slaves without Masters: The Free Negro in the Antebellum South.* New York: Vintage Books, 1976.

Billon, Frederic L. *Annals of St. Louis in Its Early Days under the French and Spanish Dominations.* St. Louis: G. I. Jones and Co., 1886.

———. *Annals of St. Louis in Its Territorial Days from 1804 to 1821.* St. Louis: For the Author, 1888.

Boyd, Robert C. "Literary Activity in Antebellum St. Louis." Ph.D. diss., Indiana University, 1989.

Bushman, Richard L. *The Refinement of America—Persons, Houses, Cities.* New York: Knopf, 1992.

Christensen, Lawrence O. "Black St. Louis: A Study in Race Relations, 1865–1916." Ph.D. diss., University of Missouri, 1972.

———. "Cyprian Clamorgan, *The Colored Aristocracy of St. Louis* (1858)." *Bulletin of the Missouri Historical Society* 31 (October 1974): 3–31.

Curry, Leonard P. *The Free Black in Urban America, 1800–1850: The Shadow of the Dream.* Chicago: University of Chicago Press, 1981.

Darby, John F. *Personal Recollections of Many Prominent People Whom I Have Known, and Events—Especially of Those Relating to the History of St. Louis—During the First Half of the Present Century.* St. Louis: G. I. Jones and Co., 1880.

Day, Judy, and M. James Kedro. "Free Blacks in St. Louis: Antebellum Conditions, Emancipation, and the Postwar Era." *Bulletin of the Missouri Historical Society* 30 (January 1974): 117–35.

Dictionary of American Biography.

Edwards, Richard, and Menra Hopewell. *Edwards' Great West and Her Commercial Metropolis, Embracing a General View of the West and a Complete History of St. Louis.* St. Louis: At the Office of Edwards' Register, 1860.

Ekberg, Carl J. *Colonial Ste. Geneviève: An Adventure on the Mississippi Frontier.* Gerald, Mo.: Patrice Press, 1985.

Fabian, Ann. *Card Sharps, Dream Books, and Bucket Shops: Gambling in Nineteenth-Century America.* Ithaca: Cornell University Press, 1990.

Fehrenbacher, Don E. *Slavery, Law, and Politics: The Dred Scott Case in Historical Perspective.* New York: Oxford University Press, 1981.

Foley, William E., and C. David Rice. *The First Chouteaus: River Barons of Early St. Louis.* Urbana: University of Illinois Press, 1983.

Gatewood, Willard B., Jr. *Aristocrats of Color: The Black Elite, 1880–1920.* Bloomington: University of Indiana Press, 1990.

Gilbert, Judith A. "Esther and Her Sisters: Free Women of Color as Property Owners in Colonial St. Louis, 1765–1803." *Gateway Heritage* 17 (summer 1996): 14–23.

Greene, Lorenzo J., Gary R. Kremer, and Antonio F. Holland. *Missouri's Black Heritage.* Rev. ed. Columbia: University of Missouri Press, 1993.

Hanchett, Catherine M. "George Boyer Vashon, 1824–1878: Black Educator, Poet, Fighter for Equal Rights." *Western Pennsylvania Historical Magazine* 68 (July 1985): 205–30, and (October 1985): 333–49.

Hogan, John. *Thoughts about St. Louis, Her Commerce and Manufactures, Railroads, &c.* St. Louis: Republican Steam Press, 1854.

Holt, Glen E. "St. Louis's Transition Decade, 1819–1830." *Missouri Historical Review* 76 (July 1982): 365–81.

Horton, James Oliver, and Lois E. Horton. *In Hope of Liberty: Culture, Community and Protest among Northern Free Blacks, 1700–1860.* New York: Oxford University Press, 1997.

Hunter, Lloyd A. "Slavery in St. Louis, 1804–1860." *Bulletin of the Missouri Historical Society* 30 (July 1974): 233–65.

Hyde, William, and Howard L. Conrad. *Encyclopedia of the History of St. Louis.* 4 vols. New York, Louisville, and St. Louis: Southern History Company, 1899.

Lapp, Rudolph M. *Blacks in Gold Rush California.* New Haven: Yale University Press, 1977.

Litwack, Leon F. *North of Slavery: The Negro in the Free States, 1790–1860.* Chicago: University of Chicago Press, 1961.

Loomis, Noel M., and Abraham P. Nasatir. *Pedro Vial and the Roads to Santa Fe.* Norman: University of Oklahoma Press, 1963.

MacGill, Caroline E., Peter Smith, et al. *History of Transportation in the United States before 1860.* N.p., 1948.

Nasatir, A. P. *Borderland in Retreat: From Spanish Louisiana to the Far Southwest.* Albuquerque: University of New Mexico Press, 1976.

———. "Jacques Clamorgan: Colonial Promoter of the Northern Border of New Spain." *New Mexico Historical Review* 17 (April 1942): 101–12.

Oglesby, Richard Edward. *Manuel Lisa and the Opening of the Missouri Fur Trade.* Norman: University of Oklahoma Press, 1963.

Primm, James Neal. *Lion of the Valley; St. Louis, Missouri.* 2d ed. Boulder, Colo.: Pruett, 1990.

Reichard, Maximilian. "Black and White on the Urban Frontier: The St. Louis Community in Transition, 1800–1830." *Bulletin of the Missouri Historical Society* 33 (October 1976): 3–17.

Richardson, Lemont K. "Private Land Claims in Missouri." *Missouri Historical Review* 50 (January, April, and July, 1956): 132–44, 271–86, 387–99.

Scharf, J. Thomas. *History of St. Louis and County, from the Earliest Periods to the Present Day, Including Biographical Sketches of Representative Men.* 2 vols. Philadelphia: Louis H. Everts and Co., 1883.

Schweninger, Loren. *Black Property Owners in the South, 1790–1915.* Urbana: University of Illinois, 1990.

Shepard, Elihu H. *The Early History of St. Louis and Missouri, from the First Exploration by White Men in 1673 to 1843.* St. Louis: Southwestern Book and Publishing Co., 1870.

Skillman, W. D. *The Western Metropolis of St. Louis in 1846.* St. Louis: W. D. Skillman, 1846.

Taylor, J. H., and M. O. Crooks. *Sketch Book of St. Louis.* St. Louis: George Knapp and Co., 1858.

Van Ravenswaay, Charles. *St. Louis: An Informal History of the City and Its People, 1764–1865.* Urbana: University of Illinois Press for the Missouri Historical Society, 1991.

Williamson, Joel. *New People: Miscegenation and Mulattoes in the United States.* New York: Free Press, 1980.

Winch, Julie. *Philadelphia's Black Elite: Activism, Accommodation, and the Struggle for Autonomy, 1787–1848.* Philadelphia: Temple University Press, 1988.

Index

About the Editor

Julie Winch has been a member of the faculty at the University of Massachusetts Boston since 1985. She has been the recipient of two National Endowment for the Humanities fellowships and has worked on various documentary projects, including PBS's *Africans in America* and The Learning Channel's genealogy program, *Who Do You Think You Are?* Other publications include *The Clamorgans: One Family's History of Race in America* and *A Gentleman of Color: The Life of James Forten.*